D1606502

Woods
We Live With

Woods
We Live With

A Guide to the Identification
of Wood in the Home

Nancy & Herbert Schiffer

Schiffer Limited
EXTON, PENNSYLVANIA

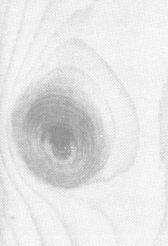

Woods We Live With

Library of Congress catalog card number: 77-92332

ISBN: 0-916838-10-2

Printed in the United States of America

To Ted and Susan

The cooperation of so many people has made it possible to present this material. We would like particularly to thank Peter Schiffer who coordinated all the research and publishing details, and Pamela Allsebrook, California Redwood Association; Caroline L. Arlington, American Forest Institute; Hal Broughton, Broughton Lumber Company; Shirley A. Brown, American Plywood Association; Elizabeth S. Busby; Linda Carlson, American Plywood Association; Rath Chantongkaew, Royal Thai Embassy; Donna J. Christensen, U.S. Forest Products Laboratory; Brooks Coburn; Frank A. Coburn; W. J. Collings, Jr., Weyerhaeuser Corporation; Gerry Cook, Caterpillar Tractor Company; W. H. Ford, Mead Paper Group; Mrs. D. M. Gardner, Western Wood Products Association; Robert E. Gorman, Caterpillar Tractor Company; Maurice E. Hobaugh, Pennsylvania Bureau of Forestry; Robert A. Holcombe, National Forest Products Association; Samuel Holtz; Gerry W. Kelly, Weyerhaeuser Corporation; Mrs. M. La France, Food and Agriculture Organization of the United Nations; Nicholas Le Pore; Harry Leslie, U.S. Forest Products Laboratory; Alan McIlvain, Alan McIlvain Company; John Maggio; Wayne Mest, Fredericks Brothers, Incorporated; Larry Miller, Champion International Corporation; Philip, Constantine and Company; Rosalind Race, Design Research; Michael J. Regen, Hardwood Plywood Manufacturers Association; Gordon Saltar, Henry Francis du Pont Winterthur Museum; Shire Publications Ltd.; Hettie M. Smith, Scott Paper Company; Ivan G. Sparks; Janice G. Spencer; Fannie M. Stokes; Gale Rawson Thompson; and Mary M. B. Wilson. Thank you.

Table of Contents

The Cooper

Many small craftsmen did not require elaborate equipment, and their margin was so slender that they would not have found it possible to support the overhead of renting a shop. In such a case they might for a small fee acquire the right to practise their craft under the arches of the gallery of some public building or large *hôtel particulier*. Or perhaps they might inherit a privilege, sometimes over many generations. Such is the arrangement of this barrel-maker, who disposes of each day's product as he makes it and whose men take their tools home with them. All he has to do is secure his benches back against the wall when night comes.

INTRODUCTION

This study is intended to identify the 48 woods most commonly used for antique and modern furniture and building construction. These woods we live with differ in visual appearance, strength, durability, workability and availability as well as expense.

In our 30 years of appraising, buying, selling and collecting antique American and European furniture, there have been mistakes in wood identification. Sometimes the errors simply caused personal disappointment as few others cared, but there have been times when a more valuable wood made the difference in the value of the furniture. Then others really did care. We constantly try to make fewer of these mistakes by simplifying the identification process.

The most common woods found in furniture will be discussed quickly in the first chapter and in greater detail when the individual woods are discussed at length. The primary and secondary woods will be considered in order to determine the probable origins of antique pieces. We have tried to keep the discussion direct. Wordy explanations seem useless when it is the eyes we must train.

The Wheelwright

All the parts of the wheel are made, and then assembled. Rim sections (Fig. 1) are mortised to receive the spokes; the spokes are mounted on the hub (Figs. 2, 3); and the sections of the rim are laid on to fit (Fig. 4). Parts are made too long for the very sound reason that it is easier to shorten than to lengthen a piece of wood. The rim is eventually mounted piece by piece on the spokes, and bound (Fig. 5) to make a solid wheel.

Chapter 1 The Woods We Live With

The world of woods is full of potentially confusing terms. By dealing with the basic ones, I hope to simplify the matter before frustration conquers. There are two general groups of trees: hardwoods and softwoods.

Hardwoods, or angiosperm, are trees that drop their broad leaves (deciduous), have support fibers, and vessels to conduct sap to the leaves. The hardwood sap vessels go like straws from the roots to the leaves, and the thickness of the support fibers determines the density of the wood. An example of a hardwood is maple.

Softwoods, or gymnosperm, are cone-bearing trees with thick tracheids that give support and thin tracheids that conduct sap. Some softwoods are harder than some hardwoods. Yellow pine (softwood) is harder than Philippine mahogany (hardwood).

In both hardwood and softwood trees, the thickness of the trunk increases as new wood is made just below the bark. This new wood has characteristic appearance, function and chemical makeup and is called sapwood. The sapwoods of different kinds of trees are each individual. The sapwood is formed in the spring and summer with greater growth, and therefore wider "rings" in the spring than in the summer. When we see the annual rings of a tree, the light colored rings are springwood and the shaded dark lines are summerwood of an annual ring.

When additional sapwood is made, the old sapwood becomes physically and chemically changed into heartwood which is usually darker in color and more compressed than sapwood.

Color differentiation between sapwood and heartwood are primary details to notice when trying to differentiate one wood from another.

BARK inner layer carries food from leaves; outer layer protects tree.

CAMBIUM layers of cells that divide to form bark and sapwood.

SAPWOOD transports water from roots to leaves.

HEARTWOOD sapwood dies, changes to strong central core.

ANNUAL RINGS Tree growth occurs in yearly layers, from top to roots.

Hardwoods can be compared with each other in density by weighing a cubic foot of wood and noting this weight relative to other hardwoods. West Indian mahogany has a weight of 50 lbs. per cubic foot, while chestnut has a weight of 30 lbs. per cubic foot. Therefore, a block of West Indian mahogany will be much heavier than the same size block of chestnut. This difference is of primary importance when considering woods for structural use in the building industry. Because of their density, some woods will support a train on a bridge, while others would send it crashing to the river below.

When thinking specifically about furniture, distinctions are made between the primary and secondary woods.

The primary woods are those that can be seen on the outside of a piece of furniture making up the sides, front and top. The secondary woods are those structural woods that are usually hidden inside.

Primary woods in the decades before mechanization were the native hardwoods and softwoods or imported woods of many varieties. Secondary woods were chosen from local woods that were easily available, inexpensive, and easily worked.

If a piece of antique furniture was made in Charleston, South Carolina, the secondary wood might be cypress. If the piece was made in New England, the secondary wood probably would be white pine. From southern New England to the southern areas of the South, one finds tulip poplar as the

HOW A TREE GROWS

Trees increase each year in height and spread of branches by adding on a new growth of twigs.

Light and heat are required by the leaves in the preparation of food obtained from the air and soil. The leaves give off moisture by transpiration.

The buds, root tips and cambium layer are the growing parts. The tree takes in oxygen over its entire surface through breathing pores on leaves, twigs, branches, trunk and roots.

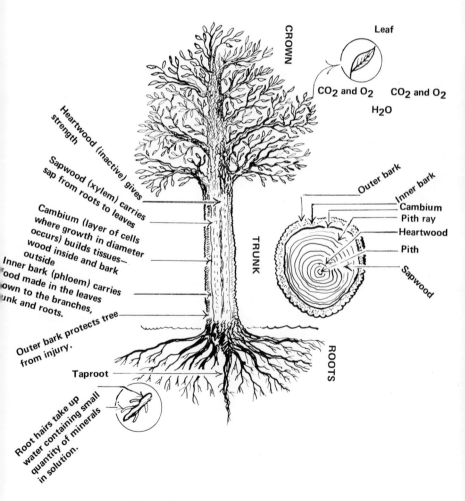

Source: Department of Environmental Resources

13

common secondary wood. White cedar often is found on drawer bottoms of furniture that was made in the Philadelphia vicinity.

Possibly when we think of fine furniture, we think first of mahogany with its rich pattern of close grain, fine color, durability and suitability for carving.

In the 16th century, the Spanish used mahogany for ship building, obtaining it in the West Indies, where logs 12 feet in diameter were found. Cuban mahogany, which was used before 1750, had a distinctive "fiddle back" curl and stripe. Cuban mahogany was lighter in color than the other West Indian types and did not darken with age.

The Santo Domingan mahogany is found primarily in fine antique furniture. It was shipped to England and the American mainland from the beginning of the 18th century.

The 1708 inventory of Charles Plumstead, a Philadelphia cabinet maker, includes mahogany. Mahogany veneers were also known at an early date. Baltimore cabinet makers used mahogany as a secondary wood in the early 19th century because it was less expensive to ship mahogany by boat from the West Indies than to obtain "local" woods by wagon on poor roads from the inlands. This problem of poor overland transportation continued everywhere until railroads were used.

Mahogany came into regular use in Charleston, South Carolina earlier than in other ports because Charleston is so close to the West Indies.

While some imported mahogany was used in the Georgia Piedmont, furniture was usually made of local walnut that came in boards 24" wide. Yellow pine (*Pinus taeda*), walnut, red maple, (*Acer rubrum*) and black cherry were the customary cabinetwoods in the inland South.

Southern yellow pine (*Pinus taeda*), also called striped pine, was used both as a primary and a secondary wood in the South, and grew North to the edge of Pennsylvania. Harry D. Green, author of *Furniture of the Georgia Piedmont* has said, "It has long been known that different growth conditions affect the color, texture and chemical compositions of various woods. The woods grown in Georgia are darker in color and have a more pronounced grain than woods (of the same tree) grown in New England. The wood gets lighter and shows less grain as we move northward". This is true; it has been said by others—forestry experts, furniture men, etc., but never has it been stated so clearly and simply.

Charles Van Ravensway has written "A Historical Checklist of the Pines of North America". This is a list of about 70 different American pines that includes information about where each grows, local and scientific names, uses, and good and bad qualities. It is a very interesting and important study.

Until quite recently, if a minor element such as a corner block on the back of a piece of antique furniture proved to be white pine, the furniture was thought to have been made in New England. However, many pieces of 18th and early 19th century American southern furniture have white pine as a secondary wood since lumber was commonly transported between New England and the South by ship. In that day, most of the vessels departing from Virginia carried lumber. Numerous advertisements for white lumber appeared in early North Carolina newspapers, and some of the furniture with southern cabinetmakers' labels that was sold in port cities has white pine secondary wood. There are still examples of old white pine paneling in Charleston homes today.

Interior paneling.

The following pictures of wood grains are arranged to be compared and contrasted with each other. Each block of wood has been cut to show three surfaces. The largest surface is the flat grained (plainsawed) surface. Below and smaller is the edge grained (quarter sawed) surface. To the left is the end grained surface.

Maple was used very commonly as a primary wood in American colonial furniture. The Pilgrims used maple for the moldings and "jewels" or bosses of court cupboards and chests.

New maple shows growth rings and pore flecks and varies considerably in grain figure. As it ages, maple becomes browner, ultimately becoming rich honey colored. Maple can be confused with birch and cherry, seen here, yet it usually has a more striped figure. Since cherry, maple and birch grow in the same areas, they are sometimes all found in a piece of antique furniture. They each can be stained to look alike.

Cherry (*Prunus serotina*) was used for antique furniture in Connecticut and New York, and is also found growing naturally in Pennsylvania, Maryland and Kentucky, just short of the deep South.

Cherry has a pinkish color that gets progressively browner with age. There are variations in the figures from stripes and lines to flecks. Cherry has a tight grain that carves beautifully and makes very attractive furniture. So much cherry furniture has been made in the Connecticut river valley that it has acquired the slang name "Connecticut mahogany."

Birch is a real chameleon of woods. When stained, birch can be made to look like maple, cherry, gum, and even walnut. It is a less expensive wood than those it resembles, so substitutions are to be expected in modern manufactured goods. Now, with accurate wood analysis possible, a good deal of antique birch furniture has been identified in the Piedmont area of Georgia.

American black walnut may be the most common and finest native cabinetmakers' wood of the mid-eighteenth century in America and early-eighteenth century in England. The wood was shipped from America to England throughout the 18th century as original bills of lading bear out, that are now housed in the British Museum. In America, at that time, black walnut furniture sold for a little less than similar pieces of mahogany.

New walnut, when wet or freshly cut, looks slightly purple. As it ages, walnut becomes grayer and browner.

Basswood has a light color with indistinct figure. Even though this softwood is easy to work, it is not recognized readily since it is usually painted, as in furniture and modern bee hives. The backs of drawers in modern furniture are sometimes made of basswood. Notice the flecking of the grain.

Tulip poplar is the easiest of this group to identify since it has characteristic green streaks. The background color varies from yellow to brown with fine flecks. Tulip poplar is soft and heavy, making it suited for structural and painted areas of furniture. Tulip poplar grows from southern New England to the Mississippi River. It has been used throughout this range as a secondary wood for drawer sides, bottoms and backs. However, as a primary wood, tulip poplar has been made into New England painted furniture, Pennsylvania dry sinks and blanket chests, painted beds, Carolina cupboards and chests of drawers.

Inventories of the 18th and 19th centuries in Chester County, Pennsylvania called for more furniture of tulip poplar than we see remaining today. The wood has a fine fleck like cherry that can resemble cherry and gum when stained. This sample is primarily green even though a large board may have only a green streak.

White cedar is resistant to bugs and water rot because of its natural oils, and therefore is used for shingles, fence posts and other outdoor uses. The wood has a yellow striped figure, sometimes with small knot holes. White cedar is sometimes found in drawer bottoms on chests made in the Delaware river valley.

Red cedar that has aged can look like cherry. It was used for furniture extensively in Bermuda, and occasionally in Newport, R.I., and Philadelphia. The wood can retain a distinct scent for many years.

Of the three similar woods shown together here, the redwood has the deepest red color, is the lightest in weight, and has the widest figure. Redwood is easily carved and because of natural resins, resists water rot. Therefore, it is ideally suited for greenhouse construction, outdoor furniture and water tanks.

Like the two other woods shown here, cypress resists water rot and is also insect resistent. The wood is browner and grayer than the redwood, but is pinker than white cedar. A board of cypress can have varying colored wood. Cypress has been found as a secondary wood in furniture from Charleston, S.C., and is used today for fences, docks, and bridges since it is relatively lightweight and durable.

Redwood log in the nineteenth century.

Ash is a strong, heavy wood rather whitish in color. It looks like chestnut, see page 44, but has larger areas of springwood (no pronounced grain) between areas of summerwood (small scratch-like lines). Ash was used in early furniture in New England for turned legs. Today, we see it as baseball bats.

Gum has a fine grain with flecking. When first cut, it looks more purple than cherry, but when it is old and faded with a bit of stain, gum is very difficult to distinguish from cherry. Gum wood has been used for over two hundred years for furniture making in the Hudson river valley, especially for Kasten and linen presses. A highboy of "bilsted" or gum that was made in New York state is now in the Winterthur Museum. Today, it is still used for furniture making.

Teak is a heavy, light brown wood when first cut, but can look white when it has been aged and sun bleached, as on boat decks. When it has been stained, teak can look like mahogany or ebony, as on old brass bound buckets. Much of the Chinese furniture we see today is made of teak.

Blue spruce

The Joiner I

By modern standards division of labor and specialization of function were still at at fairly elementary level in the 18th century. Specialization of trades, on the other hand, was carried farther than it is now and there were many more different kinds of carpenters. Carpentry proper meant gross constructions. For interior work, one would hire not a carpenter, but a joiner, whose specialty was, as the name implies, fitting different pieces and kinds of window frames or door frames, parquet floors of panelled walls. This is a joiner's yard. Two of his men are using a ripsaw.

Chapter 2 Cutting Wood

A tree is like a steer in that it has almost as many different cuts. Steak can be wasted as hamburger or shank can break your teeth when cut into small steaks.

Plain sawn or Tangential cut wood is the view of the wood you would get by looking at a tree that had been barked and flattened on your side.

Quarter sawn or radial cut wood is what you get by cutting a log on the radius.

Transverse, or end grain is obtained by slicing the tree from the top in round sections.

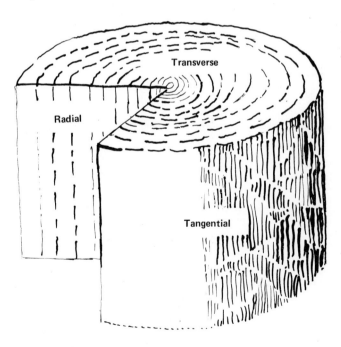

The Three Planes

Interesting grain can be revealed by cutting logs at various angles. Some of the best figured wood can be found at the crotches between the branch and the trunk, and the area near the roots can have very interesting figures.

Certain trees have large proportions of beautifully figured wood that can be exposed by cutting the logs into veneers. However, the size of a log does not indicate how much figured wood can be cut. A thick log with proportionally much less surface can yield more veneer than a longer, thinner log.

There is a story that the famous cabinetmaker Duncan Phyfe, in the early 19th century in New York, paid a thousand dollars for a mahogany log for veneers. I am sure that for the rest of his life, everyone who bought a veneered piece of furniture thought they had veneer from this log. Similarly, today, some restaurants feature champion 4-H Club steers. I hate to think how many hundreds of people think they have eaten part of a single Grand Champion steer.

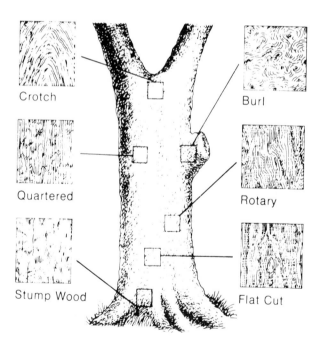

Crotch

Burl

Quartered

Rotary

Stump Wood

Flat Cut

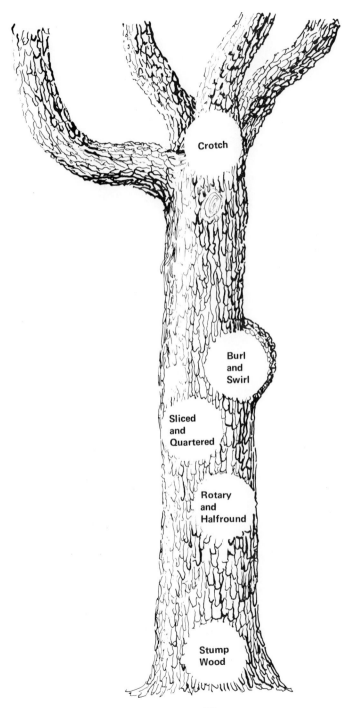

Crotch

Burl
and
Swirl

Sliced
and
Quartered

Rotary
and
Halfround

Stump
Wood

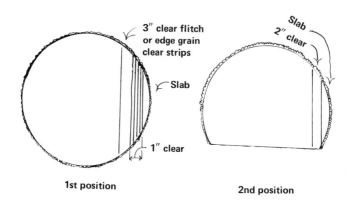

1st position

3″ clear flitch or edge grain clear strips

Slab

1″ clear

2nd position

Slab

2″ clear

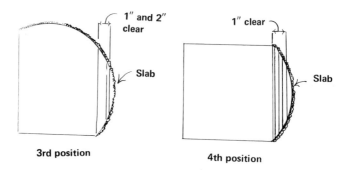

3rd position

1″ and 2″ clear

Slab

4th position

1″ clear

Slab

Cutting a log for lumber

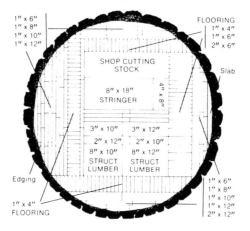

1″ x 6″
1″ x 8″
1″ x 10″
1″ x 12″

FLOORING
1″ x 4″
1″ x 6″
2″ x 6″

SHOP CUTTING STOCK

8″ x 18″ STRINGER

4″ x 8″

Slab

3″ x 10″   3″ x 12″
2″ x 12″   2″ x 10″
8″ x 10″   8″ x 12″
STRUCT   STRUCT
LUMBER   LUMBER

Edging

1″ x 4″
FLOORING

1″ x 6″
1″ x 8″
1″ x 10″
1″ x 12″
2″ x 12″

The manner in which veneers are cut is an important factor in producing the various visual effects obtained. Five principal methods of cutting veneers are used.

1. *Rotary Slicing.* The rotary lathe rotates a log against a lathe knife to produce a continuous sheet of veneer. A bold, variegated grain pattern is generally obtained in this method.

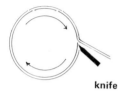

knife

2. *Flat or Plain Slicing.* A half log, or flitch, can be mounted on a lathe or slicing machine. The veneer is cut parallel to the flat side through the center of the log producing a variegated figure.

knife

3. *Half-round Slicing.* The flitch can be mounted off-center on a lathe to produce a cut across the annular growth rings. The grain shows modifications of both rotary and flat slicing.

knife

4. *Quarter Slicing.* The quarter log or flitch is cut by a knife at right angles (90°) to the growth rings. The grain is striped in some woods and variegated in others.

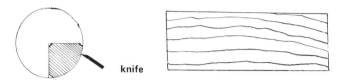

5. *Rift Cutting.* The oak quarter logs are cut at an angle of about 15% off of the quartered position, or perpendicular to the medullary rays. The resulting parallel grain pattern avoids the flake figure of the medullary rays.

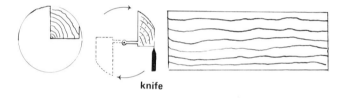

Veneer making can create more sawdust than finished inlay since there are so many cuts involved to get to the final form.

There are many ways veneers can be arranged to create interesting patterns.

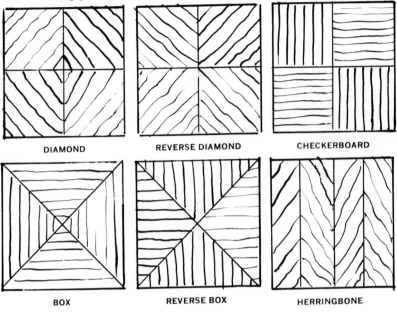

DIAMOND

REVERSE DIAMOND

CHECKERBOARD

BOX

REVERSE BOX

HERRINGBONE

Panelling can be matched in several patterns.

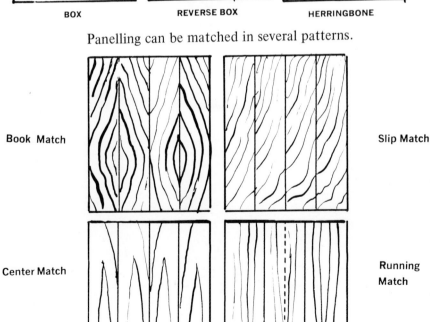

Book Match

Slip Match

Center Match

Running Match

Panel One Panel Two

Identifying the age of a veneer can help determine the age of a piece of furniture. Old hand cut veneers can be nearly 1/8″ thick and usually are well over 1/16″ thick. Since the 1840's veneers have been cut by machines to thicknesses of 1/32″ to 1/64″. (The thickness of veneer is very noticeable at the fret of a looking glass.)

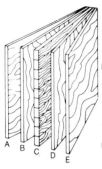

FIVE-PLY VENEER
CONSTRUCTION

A. Face veneer of fine hardwood

B. Crossband—usually poplar
   or gum

C. Core—poplar or
   particleboard

D. Crossband

E. Back veneer—to prevent
   warping

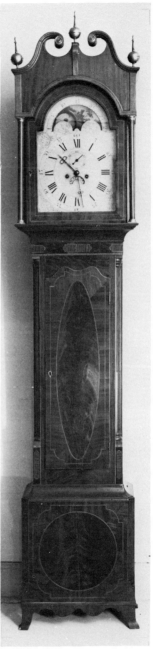

Veneer work of the 1790's brought the most carefully selected crotch grain veneers together to create decorative surfaces. This clock utilizes light stringing inlay to border the veneered panels.

33

Decorative inlays have been used on furniture for hundreds of years. Fine European examples of Renaissance marquetry pictures were made on small boxes as well as entire rooms with trompe l'oeil effects. Some of these rooms are very amusing with false books on library shelves and false doors shown open, all affected with inlayed wood. Many of the large city museums have these on display.

The woods that are so carefully chosen to produce these pictures include every type, in natural and stained colors, plain grains and exotic figures are used to simulate whatever detail the pictures require.

The making of patterned inlay is an intricate process whereby hundreds of hours can be spent figuring out how the woods are to be cut, glued, arranged, and recut to produce specific designs. Once the thinking has been done, the actual cutting is relatively straightforward.

To imagine making a few lines of diagonal patterned stringing inlay, you must first think of the colors you want at the end. Carefully chosen woods can be bleached or stained to create the proper tones. Then the individual woods are cut appropriately to the grain to prevent splitting. Glues enable the maker to arrange the wood to make up the pattern. Once the woods are placed and glued, they can be cut at a variety of angles to affect different patterns. You can think of this as making a multilayerd cake and slicing it many different ways.

Specialized patterned inlays were made and sold in small areas of America, as elsewhere, so that now these are associated with definite areas. The furniture of certain cabinetmakers can be identified or attributed sometimes on the strength of the patterned details. For example, the Seymour family of Boston in the early 19th century used a stringing inlay with round figures. Finding this inlay on furniture with stylistic designs similar to their other work and with a Boston lineage could probably help to attribute the furniture to the Seymour workshop.

Now technology is being applied to the tool field to find a steel that can be very thin, yet strong enough to cut veneers. Thinner saws will make less sawdust and less waste for this specialized field.

Boxwood and holly are woods well suited to the inlay making business as they are very even and light grained, and are strong enough to hold the small detail of cut work.

Shaded tones from light to dark on the same piece of wood can be made by placing light wood in very hot sand where the wood will slowly burn and darken. By frequently checking the wood, the color and depth of darkness can be controlled.

Holly wood is inlayed into this walnut chest to make the vine, leaf and berry designs. The striped, cross grain veneer around the drawers is probably hickory.

This American desk was made around 1780 of black walnut with cherry and possibly birch inlay. The design is probably unique.

Plywood construction

Plywood is a structural material manufactured by bonding sheets of wood together with the grains of adjacent layers at right angles to one another.

Fig. 1 At the mill, logs are separated and stacked by wood species. They may also be sorted by length and grade quality before they are cut into peeler blocks.

Fig. 2 Bark, removed from the log, is used as garden mulch or fuel at the plant to provide power. Bark can be removed by a high pressure water jet, chipped off by knurled wheels or peeled off with knives.

Fig. 3 The last premanufacturing step in plywood production is to cut the peeler blocks, which are sections of log that will fit the veneer-cutting lathes. Peeler blocks are 8′ 4″ long. Blocks are usually soaked in a hot water vat or steamed before peeling.

Fig. 4 Peelable block next travels to a lathe spotter and charger. The spotter elevates and levels the block to the charger. The charger then moves the block forward to lathe chucks which will hold the block against the lathe knife.

Fig. 5 Lathe chucks revolve the block against a long knife which peels a continuous thin ribbon of veneer at up to 600 lineal feet per minute. Softwood veneer is usually peeled in thicknesses ranging from 1/10″–1/4″.

Fig. 6 Clippers cut the veneer ribbon into usable widths (up to 54″) and cut out sections with nonrepairable defects. Veneers are dried in ovens as much as 100 feet long to a moisture content of about 5%, then are sorted by grade.

Fig. 1

Fig. 2

Fig. 3

Fig. 4

Fig. 5

Fig. 6

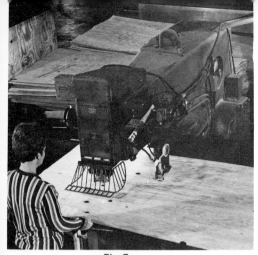

Fig. 7

Fig. 8

Fig. 9

Fig. 10

Fig. 7 Small defects, such as knotholes, are removed by diecutting; the holes are filled with patches, which may be oval or boat shaped. Grain of wood patches runs the same direction as that of the veneer. Synthetic patches are also used in repairing panels.

Fig. 8 After drying and patching, veneer sheets are glued and sandwiched together in one continuous operation.

Fig. 9 The veneer sandwiches travel to the hot press, where they are loaded into racks for bonding under heat and pressure. Generally, the heat range is 230°F to 315°F, and the pressure ranges from 175 to 200 pounds per square inch.

Fig. 10 Rough plywood panels are then trimmed to size, sanded (if required), graded and stamped. Finished panels will move by railroad car or truck to building supply wholesalers and distributors.

38

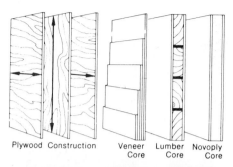

Plywood Construction   Veneer   Lumber   Novoply
                         Core   Core   Core

U S PLYWOOD PRODUCTS USED IN RESIDENTIAL CONSTRUCTION

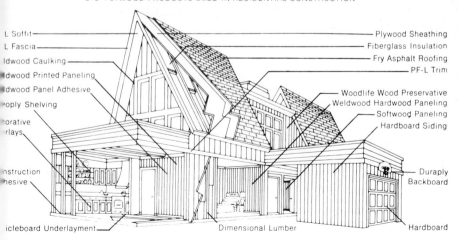

L Soffit —
L Fascia —
ldwood Caulking —
ldwood Printed Paneling —
ldwood Panel Adhesive —
oply Shelving —
corative
rlays —
nstruction
hesive —
icleboard Underlayment —

— Plywood Sheathing
— Fiberglass Insulation
— Fry Asphalt Roofing
— PF-L Trim
— Woodlife Wood Preservative
— Weldwood Hardwood Paneling
— Softwood Paneling
— Hardboard Siding
— Duraply
— Backboard

Dimensional Lumber

— Hardboard

39

Carpentry

Carpentry was a vigorous and fundamental trade. (a) sawing timbers, (b) chiseling mortises, (c) squaring joints, (d) trimming down a beam. The foreman (e) is instructed by the master-builder, and the workman (f) does many of the jobs around the yard. The shed (h) affords some comfort in the rain. To the left is a timbered front (i) to be plastered. A more advanced lumber scaffolding (k) is used for masonry construction.

Chapter 3 Problems of Wood Identification in Furniture

Someone recently told me he had most of the problems of authenticating old furniture solved. I asked how it was so simple. He responded that many of the woods found in lumber yards today did not grow in the original 13 colonies, such as western pines. This is true. He went on, that if a drawer side in a chest of drawers, that was supposedly made in Philadelphia in 1770, turned out to be Douglas fir, the chest could not be authentic. Well, that was his theory. Unfortunately, it is of very limited use because a competent cabinetmaker restoring an antique piece would use appropriate antique wood to make any repairs. An incompetent cabinetmaker's work would probably be so inferior that there would be no question of authenticity to begin with, and the age of new repair wood would be obvious.

Identifying the type, age, and finish on wood can be a challenging operation, since many variables combine to give wood its appearance.

A lot of nonsense has been spoken by oldtimers who quickly assume knowledge of wood identification. "If wood has worm holes, it is English." There are also worms in America, the West Indies, and many other parts of the world. "I can tell by eye American from English oak." This difference cannot be determined by the eye alone. "The differences can't be told in a laboratory most of the time." Modern microscopic analysis and research usually can determine the specific type of wood. "I can tell southern pine from Scotch pine." These two are extremely difficult to differentiate, even with modern methods.

For a great many of the day-to-day activities where wood identification is necessary, a general knowledge of wood types is sufficient. Characteristics that are apparent to the eyes distinguish most woods from each other. Because color is an important identifying characteristic, the natural colors of freshly cut surfaces have been reproduced on the follow-

41

ing pages. The grain patterns are shown from three surfaces of each wood. The largest surface is the flat grained (plain-sawed) surface. Below and smaller is the edge grained (quarter sawed) surface. To the left is the end grained surface.

These three woods look enough alike to be confusing, but their growing habits help to differentiate them.

Yellow pine is red-yellow toned with dark red, wide summerwood stripes. This wood easily can be confused with a striped pine from the British Isles. In America, it is found as both a primary and a secondary wood on antique furniture in the South, southeastern Pennsylvania, and Delaware.

Sugar pine is light pink with short brown streaks. The wood is lightweight, straight grained, and easy to work. Today, it is used as a construction wood, for interior finishes, and for pattern work for metal castings. Since it grows in the Cascade Mountain range of Washington state, it is never found on old furniture.

Douglas fir wood is pinkish-brown with well defined stripes that could be confused with yellow pine. The Douglas fir wood, however, is less red. This is an important wood today for plywood construction, and it can be used for a wide range of products from interior trim to railroad ties.

Ponderosa pine

43

These three woods are similar enough to be mistaken for one another.

Hickory usually has uniform striping that covers the entire surface. The rays look like etched lines at the lower edge of the plainsawed section. Old hickory can be confused with chestnut, seen below, and is often found in American Windsor chairs. Hickory is almost twice as heavy as chestnut. On a large sample, the weight may aid in differentiating the two.

Chestnut wood is a little darker than ash, but browner than hickory. The annual rings have wide springwood and compacted, darker summerwood with pores that again, look like etched lines. Chestnut is a medium heavy wood.

Oak is tight grained, heavy and strong. The wood looks like chestnut, hickory and ash, but is grayer. They all have the distinct pores. Oak has medullary rays which radiate from the center of the log like the spokes of a wheel, and appear as long, thin, uncolored lines usually perpendicular to the grain. See page 157 for a look at these rays on the birdcage frame. Since oak is so hard, it ages slowly, keeping a sharp edge on corners of drawers, for example, and chisels to cut it must be beveled at a particular angle and sharpened often.

White oak

This page shows the same 4″ square block of cherry wood sanded and turned to show the four different surfaces. The left column has been varnished clear to intensify the grain. Old cherry has a still darker color.

Many amateur, and sadly, many full-time cabinetmakers and repairers power sand, scrape or otherwise remove the old surface when they try to refinish a piece of old, oxidized furniture. They make the pieces look "new," and in some cases make it difficult to identify an old piece without inspecting the unfinished surfaces. Their work invariably cuts the value of the furniture a great deal.

A mellow appearance comes with age. If an old surface has become opaque, as on fine oil paintings, the old varnish can be removed and replaced with a clear protective coating, but the painting should not be cleaned down to the canvas. So, too, with wood.

Black cherry

Here we see how various stains can alter the appearance of the four most prominent primary woods. From top to bottom, the rows show mahogany, cherry, walnut, and maple boards, all cut at least 150 years ago.

The woods in the left column are unfinished old surfaces. A clear varnish has been applied to the wood in the second column. The third column has been darkened with a walnut stain. A cherry stain has been applied to the wood in the last column.

Many pieces of furniture and paneling have only clear varnish on the wood, so wood with colors like these will be familiar.

Walnut stain is used to make mahogany, cherry and maple browner, as often they look richer and bolder with the darker tone.

Cherry stain gives walnut a richer, warmer, redder appearance. On maple, cherry stain makes the wood very difficult to identify from actual cherry with a clear varnish.

Black walnut

Here is additional evidence of the chameleon quality of birch. These are five samples from the same birch board with different stained surfaces.

The top sample has clear varnish and was chosen to show the fleck that looks like cherry and maple.

The second sample is birch colored with walnut stain, making it very difficult to identify from actual walnut. If a small piece were cut into, the birch would look white while walnut would look purple.

The middle sample is birch with cherry stain. Since the wood has many of the dark pores typical of birch, this one may not fool everyone, but the color is an acceptable "antique cherry."

The fourth sample has mahogany stain and would be very difficult to identify from actual mahogany. If a small cut were made into this wood, it would like white, while actual mahogany would look pink.

The bottom sample shows both flecking at the center and dark pores at the edges. A maple stain has made the birch look so much like real maple that most people would be fooled. The dark pores at the edges resemble bleached mahogany with this color.

Today, many pieces of furniture in museums are being re-labeled as tests are being conducted to establish the actual wood types. Many pieces of furniture that previously were called other woods are turning out to be birch.

Birch

These are the three principal secondary woods found on American colonial furniture. These pieces of wood were cut at least 150 years ago. The top row is yellow pine (striped pine, *Pinus taeda*). The row across the middle is tulip poplar, and the row across the bottom is white pine (*Pinus strobus*).

The blocks in the left column each have been gently sanded to expose the figure of the wood. The blocks in the central column show old surfaces that might be found inside the drawers or back of a chest of drawers. Some oxidation is evident here. The blocks in the right column have been taken from fully oxidized wood such as the outside back or bottom of a chest. These exterior areas were also subject to impurities from wood burning fires and later coal fires that deepen the tone of the surface.

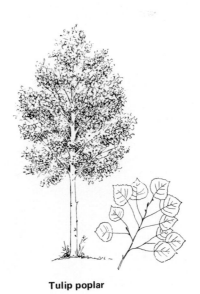

Tulip poplar

These are the oxidized samples of the four most common primary woods found in American antique furniture. Each sample is over 150 years old. The rows from top to bottom show walnut, mahogany, maple, and cherry samples.

Unfinished old surfaces are shown in the left column. This is how each wood looks with minimal oxidation such as at the back side of drawer fronts, under chest tops, and inside the sides of a case piece. The central column shows each wood with an old clear varnished surface. The right column shows each with an old oxidized surface.

The old opaque finishes on the walnut and mahogany samples are terrible. None of the wood grain is visible. It is not desirable to "skin" or over refinish these surfaces, but with these old dirty finishes carefully removed and then protected by a clear finish, a far more attractive surface could be seen. The old maple finish is quite pleasing and might simply be protected by some natural wax. The cherry sample could be gently cleaned and protected with clear finish.

Maple

These further examples show oxidation changing the appearance of wood.

The top row is butternut, middle row gum, and the bottom row walnut.

The left column shows a sanded surface whereby the natural grain is visible. The second column has aged about 150 years with no stains or varnish. The third column shows old surfaces that have simply been coated with clear varnish to bring out the grains.

The last column shows old finishes that have turned opaque from oxidation and soil over the years.

Butternut was used for furniture quite a lot in the 18th century. It carves well and is easier to work than walnut. Since butternut and walnut can look very similar, it may be important sometime to distinguish one from another. To do this, a small cut can be made in the wood at the back of a drawer or inside a foot. If the wood is butternut, the cut will look yellow-white. If it is walnut, it will look purple.

Gum is a redder wood than butternut, with a plainer grain that looks like cherry.

The freshly sanded walnut sample has a purple cast. The old surface is rather gray, and when clear varnished becomes rich brown. The opaque surface, however, has gone dull, dark and dead. Coal dust with its sulfur residue and wood ash with grease and creosote turn old varnished surfaces pale and opaque.

Cypress

57

Woods appear differently in furniture after having been aged 100 or more years. The deeper, richer colors are due partly to oxidation, and partly to dirt from heating methods. Wood fires give a tobacco leaf color and coal tar gives a still darker color with gray and green tinges from the sulphur. This coal dirt is more frequently seen on English furniture which in the 19th century was exposed to coal dust.

Since all parts of the same piece of furniture do not get the same amount of exposure to air, the wood will change color at different rates. The color of the bottom of a chest of drawers will be far darker than that of the back of the drawers.

A looking glass hangs out from the wall at the top. The backboard is usually darker at the top than the bottom due to the air circulation and dirt deposits.

The common secondary woods pine and poplar, which are relatively not dense, show age quite early; it takes far longer for oak, which is dense, to show age.

There is a strange phenomenon called a horizon line which appears at the junction of two aged and oxidized pieces of wood which meet at right angles. At the junction there is a line of slightly lighter colored wood. Glue impregnates the wood here and causes the wood to be protected from the air. This is intensified by air circulation patterns that do not get into this area to darken the wood as much as the wood around it. When boards have been darkened with stains rather than years of exposure to air, they usually build up "dirt" in the junction area. Therefore, these areas of union between two boards will be darker than the surrounding wood.

Bleaching

The strongest bleach on finished wood is sunlight. A piece of furniture that has a lovely mellow color was placed in a sunny window. After several weeks a candlestick was moved and the wood around it had bleached sufficiently that the silhouette of the candlestick clearly stood out.

The English prize naturally bleached walnut and mahogany antique furniture. Many mahoganys and walnuts are naturally dark, yet bleach with sunlight. When making repairs on bleached wood, surfaces that must be sanded become darker and the cabinetmaker must chemically bleach them to the lighter tone of the surrounding wood.

Bleaching is done intentionally occasionally when the woods in a piece of furniture vary a great deal in color and the overall effect is very dark. However, if a piece of furniture is too light, stain can be applied to mellow the color.

Paint

Many pieces of furniture, such as Windsor chairs, were made of suitable rather than attractive woods and were always painted.

Yellow pine southern furniture also was painted, as were New England softwoods that were made into furniture. It wasn't until the modern age when wood became important and the public wanted to see the wood. (People always admire what they don't have.)

The commonest colors found on painted furniture are Spanish brown, black, red, green, yellow, gray and blue. With interesting color contrasts and decorative schemes, painted furniture can disguise an otherwise simple piece of ordinary wood into something quite remarkable.

The Pennsylvania Germans simulated ornate inlay with painted decoration on their furniture, and are particularly well known for blanket chest designs. The paint on this pine chest is so thin that the natural wood grain is perceptible beneath. The sides and area between the front panels are painted to simulate hardwood grains.
Repainted chests usually have thick paint which spoils the original, spontaneous decoration.

Grain painted furniture was also fashionable in the 19th century. In rural regions especially, where the transportation of imported wood overland was too costly to be practical, ingenious painters simulated mahogany, ebony and satinwood on local woods. These attempts to fool the eye are now appreciated in their own right and considered charming examples of folk art.

Paint has cleverly concealed this softwood chest with elaborate grain decoration. This practice was common in rural areas where hardwoods were unavailable, so artists became skilled at simulating ornate grains.

The wide range of painted softwood furniture is exhibited in this room setting.

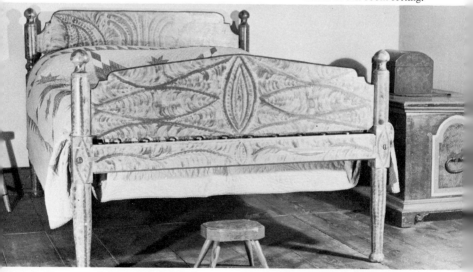

Examples of 18th and 19th century interior marbleizing and paneling are at many prominent museums. When the fashionable people couldn't have actual marble, they concealed wood paneling with painted representations of marble.

Marbleized pillars at the Atheneum in Philadelphia.

Shrinkage

As wood dries it naturally shrinks more across the grain than lengthwise.

Shrinkage will cause stress on the wood, and where the wood is held firm, cracks will form. This can happen over a long period or just a few weeks. If a room has been moist, due to open windows in the summer, and suddenly the windows are closed and the heat turned on, the wood in that room may dry out quickly. Certain places are most apt to crack: next to nails, dovetails, or mortises.

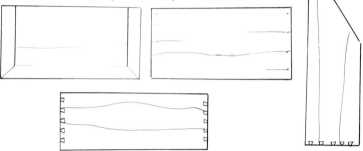

In these illustrations, the slant board of the desk is cracked at the mortise; the sides of the box are cracked at the nails; and the drawer and desk sides are cracked at the dove tails.

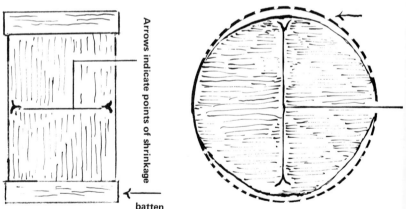

Arrows indicate points of shrinkage

batten

Originally the battens were flush with the edge of the top. The main board has shrunk across the grain.

The dotted line is the original round shape. The solid line is the shrinkage across the grain, as on all antique round table tops.

62

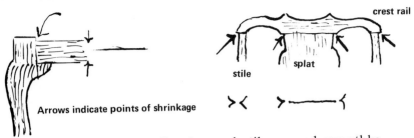

crest rail

stile

splat

Arrows indicate points of shrinkage

Originally the crest rail, splat, and stiles curved smoothly together. Now there is a noticeable gap caused by shrinkage across the grain of the stiles and splat. The crest rail does not shrink noticeably lengthwise.

Originally the seat rail was level with the top of the leg. Now a separation is due to vertical shrinkage across the grain in the seat rail.

Shrinkage can be a tool for the antiquarian in helping to determine the age of furniture. When two boards have their grains at right angles, shrinkage over the years will cause the end grain of one board to project above the tangential grain of the other board.

Therefore, an old chair will have the legs projecting above the seat rail, and the crest rail will overhang the stiles and slat. Antique "round" topped tables are no longer round after 150 years. The average 33″ diameter tea table top that was round when it was turned has by now shrunk three quarters of an inch out of round. Old bed posts, turned legs, pedestals, etc. are all out of round, but they are not as noticeable as the table top. Shrinkage can be measured on a bed post with calipers.

Characteristic shrinkage and distortion of flat, square, and round cuts are affected by the direction of the annual rings. Tangential shrinkage is about twice as great as radial.

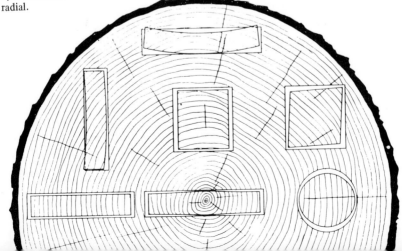

Beautifully grained hardwood veneers are fixed to secondary woods such as pine for strength. The differences in the shrinking properties of the veneers and backing woods sometimes causes structural problems in the furniture. For example, the crest of a looking glass may be mahogany veneer on pine. Since the pine is much more susceptible to shrinkage than mahogany, the crest will eventually become curved toward the wall in a dry atmosphere. The piece has not been ruined however. It will expand again and almost straighten out in the next humid season.

Hepplewhite furniture is commonly veneered and likely to have a bulging surface, or at a more advanced stage, peel, due to changes in the shrinkage of its woods. Therefore, repair costs for veneered furniture are always more than for solid-built furniture since the time and patience of a skilled cabinetmaker is required to correct veneer problems.

Cracks

Cracks are sometimes filled invisibly with thin slivers of the same type of wood as the cracked board. This method of repair is frowned upon by some cabinetmakers, however, because high humidity can cause the repaired wood as well as the board to swell, causing additional cracking or warpage. An alternative repair method is the use of "stick shellac" or pencil-like bars of wax colored to match wood types. These waxes are not noticeable when correctly blended to match the cracked board and applied in the proper manner. Now when high humidity swells the board, the wax will be pushed up like a mole hill, and this can be leveled by scraping the crack gently with a plastic credit card.

Moldings

Mouldings are used on furniture for both constructional and decorative purposes. The principal constructional use is for hiding dovetails, the intertwined joint of two planks at right angles. These can be seen at the tops of chest of drawers. Decorative moldings give many pieces charm and a change of depth that make the pieces sculptural. Shadows caused by moldings can help to make graceful transitions between surfaces. Highboys exemplify this detail with the waist moldings being structural and decorative between the upper and lower cases. Purely decorative moldings appear on chests from New England made in the Pilgrim style. These turnings have no structural function, but they enliven the surface and cast shadows that give the impression of depth.

Knowledge of where woods naturally grew, plus the ability to recognize them, helps to pin down the place where a piece of furniture is likely to have been made.

This magnificent small chest of drawers proves its place of manufacture and authenticity when examined as an appraiser, dealer, museum curator or collector should do.

The outside appearance is enhanced by natural aging, staining and finishing and can be very deceiving but begging to tell you the truth.

The mahogany case actually could be stained walnut on the outside. Look at the inside of the drawers. If necessary, cut a small piece inside. Mahogany will be pink.

Next, look at the "dust lining" drawer separations.

Tulip poplar is generally found as a secondary wood in the Middle Atlantic states, yet Newport, R.I. cabinetmakers also used it. The drawer guides are yellow pine (*Pinus taeda*). The Delaware river valley is the most northern growth limit of yellow pine.

Now examine the drawers. The sides are of tulip poplar wood. The bottoms are white cedar which grew in New Jersey bogs near Philadelphia. The drawer bottoms of many fine Philadelphia pieces of furniture in the late Queen Anne and Chippendale periods are made of white cedar, including many of the most elaborately carved highboys and lowboys. This white cedar—a wood looking like pine but with small knots and a tendency to lift rather than plane perfectly smooth— is a local Philadelphia characteristic. The drawer sides and backs are both tulip poplar, while the bottom of the case and the braces to the back feet are yellow pine.

Thus, this piece's origin must be the junction of the growing areas for pine, white cedar, and tulip poplar. The mahogany was imported from the West Indies by ship. Since freight rates on land were enormous, the mahogany was used right at the seaport. Therefore, Philadelphia is this chest's probable place of construction.

Eighteenth and 19th century Windsor chairs were originally painted. Their woods were selected for their best use rather than their appearance.

The crest rails usually are oak, chestnut or hickory which are strong.

The spindles are hickory as they have strength and some flexibility.

The legs are maple, chestnut or oak which turn well.

The seats are white pine in New England, and tulip poplar in Pennsylvania, Delaware and New Jersey, which are easy woods to shape and carve.

This chair has a crest rail of oak, the spindles are hickory, the seat is tulip poplar, and the legs are maple. These woods were all found in Pennsylvania—the origin of the chair.

Kasten and cupboards on chests made from the Hudson river valley into New Jersey sometimes look as though they were made of cherry wood, but almost always the wood is gum. Aged gum with a little varnish or wax is very hard to differentiate from cherry. (The secondary wood is tulip poplar.) The cupboard on chest shown here was probably made near New Brunswick, New Jersey.

The next kas was made of gum wood, and shows a strong Dutch influence in the overall design. The bold cornice and large, turned feet are typical of the New York style. This kas comes from the Hudson river valley.

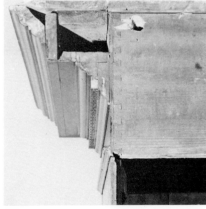

Whereas the previous kas is typically German (or Dutch) in feeling, this cherry kas is a Pennsylvania Quaker interpretation with the addition of the drawers. The mellow cherry grain is contrasted with bold fluting and a wall of troy molding. Cherry wood carves well and holds the carved edges sharply. A detail of the cornice molding shows six separate parts that combine to create it.

72

American black walnut is the primary wood on this superb semi-high chest of drawers. The back is pine and shows the drawer dividers mortised through. An early feature of construction is the use of a single board to form the side of the case and foot block, with decorative molding applied to the outside.
The drawer bottoms are white cedar.
The chest was made near Philadelphia.

Simpla table with two leaves made for Design Research in France of beech.

Butcherboard table made of assorted northern hardwood—birch, beech or maple—in the United States.

Director chair made of kiln dried hardwood in the United States.

Cultural lag is a term used to describe the use of "old fashioned" methods and styles long after their prominent time. Areas far from the cultural centers can be 30 to 70 years behind in cultural development.

Here an English sawyer was working about 1900. Even today Tanzanian workers cut timber from logs with a pit saw, as reported in the *Wall Street Journal* of October 11, 1977.

For example, this picture taken about 1901 shows men using a pit-saw in rural England. Power sawmills had been used elsewhere for over 60 years by that date. However, rural shipyards continued to cut boards with pit-saws that had been the only means of sawing lumber in the pre-mechanized period. The same thing happens with furniture styles.

A matching highboy and lowboy at the Winterthur Museum are examples of the style of 1720, but were made in a culturally conservative area in 1803.

The Cabinetmaker

Since the 18th century the tools and methods of the carpenter-builder have evolved in just that direction of lightness and precision toward which they were urged by the Encyclopedists. The cabinetmaker's techniques have changed much less. Indeed, when department store furniture is compared to what could be bought by customers of comparable establishments in the 18th century, it is clear that the changes involves the deterioration of a trade, not its development.

The plate represents a cabinetmaker's workroom, strewn with tools and materials in that state of disorder which sometimes bespeaks confident craftsmanship.

CUTTING WOOD SPECIMENS FOR MICRO-EXAMINATION

Sometimes unusual and difficult woods must be professionally analyzed to determine their species.

Wood can be analyzed for the public at the Henry Francis duPont Winterthur Museum, Winterthur, Delaware or at the Forest Products Laboratory, Madison, Wisconsin.

A sample should be taken according to these recommendations prepared by Gordon Salter, the wood specialist at the Winterthur Museum.

The Ideal Specimen

The ideal specimen is a compact little block without any crack or split, worm-hole or decay, taken from an area of straight grain, not close to any knot or suggestion of burl. From it, each of the planes illustrated can be sectioned and examined.

A specimen such as a long splinter may contain as much as .5 cc of good wood; but lacking a transverse plane. It may be difficult or impossible to identify.

A specimen cut in the following way is usually *worthless.* It can yield no plane except a hundred or so internal ruptures which parallel the plane of the knife blade. Only by sheer coincidence might these planes be of radial or tangential plane. Small shavings are usually worthless.

The Best Blade

The best tool generally available for taking specimens is a strong-handled, good steel (not stainless) pocket knife, stout through the blade, thinning toward the point and *razor sharp.* Kept in good shape by frequent honings on the oil stone, this tool will take the best specimens with least damage to the object under study.

Razor blades are next to worthless except the "Weck" which can serve as auxilliary to a good knife in many cases. You still need the knife.

How To Cut

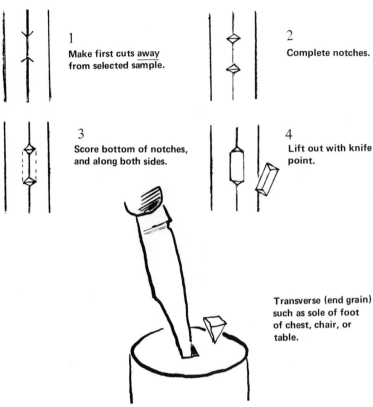

1
Make first cuts away from selected sample.

2
Complete notches.

3
Score bottom of notches, and along both sides.

4
Lift out with knife point.

Transverse (end grain) such as sole of foot of chest, chair, or table.

Where To Cut

Sometimes a piece of "mahogany" furniture may have a rear rail, rear legs, or other parts which turn out to be walnut. This is a stroke of fortune since under the microscope the European and American walnut can usually be identified.

Normally, however, the secondary woods are the ones to be sampled: glued corner blocks, drawer bottoms, backs, sides, back panels, shelves, etc.

Sampling primary woods is less easy, but using discretion good specimens can be taken from the soles of feet, from beneath escutcheons, the lower edge of drawer fronts, the underside of tops, rails, arms, etc.

Size

Specimens the size of .5 cc are excellent, or the size of a pencil eraser. Only too often the largest that can be taken is not much larger than a grain of wheat. Frequently we get good results, but the chance of accurate determination of many species of wood is greatly reduced.

There are certain genera which nearly always require a larger sample for species identification, that is oaks, chestnuts, beeches, ashes, and tilias (limes, lindens, and bass woods). Often small blocks of these as large as 2 or 3 cc are sent to the laboratory and are, of course, returned afterwards to be glued back into their original positions.

Embedding

Embedding of specimens is a commendable laboratory technique (in the laboratory), and no doubt is done with the best intentions—to prepare the specimen for use in a microtome and to insure against being shattered by our postal services. However, by the time the embedding compound is dissolved and boiled out of the wood tissue, little remains of its original lustre, hue, or capacity to fluoresce under ultraviolet; and these factors cannot be gauged at all while the fibers are saturated with waxes or resins—factors which may be essential to a final determination.

Mailing

Specimens generally seem to travel safely in the mail if padded well with soft packing material and the envelope labeled *PLEASE HAND STAMP* (in red). If the specimen is very fragile, several layers of cardboard taped together with a center hole cut to fit will provide added protection.

But remember, a well cut little block travels best. *And keep the knife sharp!*

Special Cases

Take specimen from the bottom of a foot only as a last resort for it is usually full of impurities and sometimes decay.

To determine the geographic origin of beech, cherry, maple, larch, and the northern pines requires a large *tangential* plane of three to four square centimeters.

To determine the geographic origin of chestnut, birch, ash, hackberry and elm requires a large *transverse* plane of three square centimeters.

It is important *not* to take a specimen from any area near a knot for in that area there will be too much distortion of the cellular structure.

In the case of the northern pines (Scots and red), larch and beech it is important *not* to take a specimen from adolescent wood. That is to say, from within 2-2/1" of the pith, because the young tree of less than 5" diameter would rarely have developed the cell structure of adult wood necessary for its species' identification.

This puts a burden of some care upon him, who cuts the specimen; but any cabinetmaker or person of woodworking experience should find it no great challenge. Anyone else had better take samples from two or more places to be safe.

Chapter 4 Forest Management

The forest represents the climax of a long succession of natural processes. Light, temperature, moisture and soil provide the conditions in which plant life grows—and each tree has slightly different conditions required for its maximum growth. The management of these conditions can affect the type and quality of the wood grown.

In the 19th century exploitation of forests was never questioned as the supply seemed inexhaustible. Loggers went through the forests felling trees, and were followed by buckers who trimmed the branches and bucked, or cut, the tree into lengths suitable for the saw mills. Teams of oxen and horses moved gigantic logs.

All winter, these logs would sit until melting snow filled the rivers with water on which the logs rode to the mills downstream. With this lumber cities were built, the world economy grew and technology advanced faster than ever before.

In Thailand, elephants were taught when young to drag teak logs with their trunks and tusks.

Gradually, mechanized methods replaced the animal and man power in most areas. There are still areas where animals are more practical than machines. Steam locomotives powered by waste wood moved logs from deep in the valleys and mountains. Of course, hours of man power were needed initially to build the railways and bridges but eventually the locomotives were economical.

Ice and water flumes are used in some places to move logs and lumber downhill.

Another method for moving logs is the use of spar trees. Tall, straight, solidly rooted trees near the railroad lines and logging roads are chosen to haul felled timber from inaccessible areas. Guy lines are attached to give greater stability, and wires rigged by pulleys to a steam powered engine lift the logs to railway cars and trucks. A skilled logger must climb the spar tree and cut off the top so the tree will not sway while being used. Since tremendous backlash flips these trees around when the top snaps, it is a brave, strong man who makes the cut, and clings to the tree for his life as it whips back. The logs are then hauled by these wires to railway cars and trucks.

The following chart demonstrates the growing rate of the use of paper board per man per year in our dynamic 20th century.

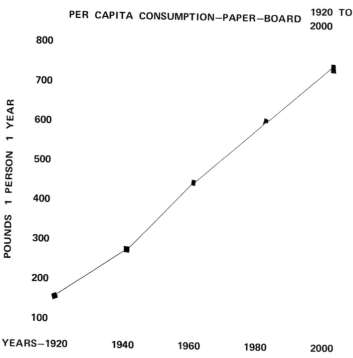

PER CAPITA CONSUMPTION—PAPER—BOARD 1920 TO 2000

The ballooning demand for wood products can be met if the world's commercial forests are allowed to be professionally managed. Through such techniques as thinning, fertilization, disease and insect control, genetic selection and breeding of superior trees, plus harvest methods suited to the site and species, managed forests can produce at least 30% more than an unmanaged stand.

Modern forest management is based on numerous specialties, such as forest pathology, wildlife biology, entomology, tree genetics and forest soil analysis. Specialists in these fields have contributed in developing current logging practices.

There are three primary methods of managing a tree farm. These methods all can be used on a single farm depending on many variable conditions.

Seed-tree Method: When an area has randomly been seeded from the forest, it can be thinned to leave desirable seed-trees standing only. Later, the area may need thinning again when crowded seedlings compete for the light and water.

In nature, seeding is a random process with the percentage of seeds that germinate and mature very low. In professionally managed forests with reforestation methods that oversee each stage of development, the percent of seeds that reach maturity is much higher.

Two trees of the same age illustrate the benefits of forest management. The smaller tree was grown on unmanaged land while the larger tree was grown in the same climate and soil conditions on land that was periodically thinned This method takes more man power than the clear-cut method with natural seedlings.

Single Tree Selection Method: Trees are selected of all sizes from all areas of the forest for cutting. Natural hardwood stands tend to be crowded with mature trees inhibiting new growth. Thinning provides some wood for the wood industry, and enables light to reach younger trees that will grow. After about 20 years, a new harvest of the mature trees will again thin the stand and allow young trees to grow. When they are hauled out of the forest, some are sent for lumber, some for pulp, etc., depending on their quality and size. This method is most expensive initially, but the forest balance is not upset.

HARDWOOD FOREST MANAGEMENT

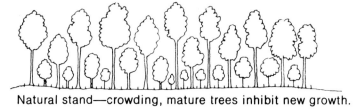

Natural stand—crowding, mature trees inhibit new growth.

Thinning—provides wood for use, releases light for growth.

20 years—ready for 2nd harvest, new growth cycle underway.

Trees are selected and marked for cutting.

Clear Cutting Method: The area of land is completely cleared of all trees. This open area can then be planted with new seedlings or allowed to re-seed naturally from the surrounding forest.

Almost ten times as many seedlings of a crop tree are planted than are expected to be harvested when mature, since some will be choked out by other growth, others eaten by animals, or some even killed by disease or natural disasters.

Softwood seedlings are planted in rows wide enough to allow plenty of room for the mature trees. By trimming limbs on the growing trees, larger quantities of first grade wood can be ensured. After about 30 years, the seedlings are mature for harvest. The area then can be clear cut again and prepared for new seedlings.

Clearcut areas that are left unseeded will become eroded, and ruined. Erosion protection and wildlife habitats are planned from the surrounding forest.

SOFTWOOD FOREST MANAGEMENT

Seedlings planted in well spaced rows for growing space.

30 years—stand ready for harvest, size, maximum yield.

Site prepared, superior seedlings for maximum growth.

A clearcut area in central Pennsylvania.

The clearcut area is carefully tilled. This special plow builds the soil into long mounds and cuts a furrow where the young seedlings will be planted.

Workers in Paraguay fertilize three-month-old pine seedlings.

Douglas fir seedlings are planted in the northwestern United States.

More and more woodland owners, including huge industries, national and state governments and individuals, are growing trees as a crop. Each year tree nurseries raise almost a billion seedlings and the forest industry plants more than a half million acres in the farming cycle. Thus, wood is grown and regrown in a cycle of harvest and planting.

Nurseries throughout timberland areas are constantly working to develop superior trees with high yields of wood and better use of land. Breeding methods as well as forest management are investigated in the search which has produced dramatic results already.

A new forest begins to grow.

Strong seedlings that grow rapidly are developed to have resistance to natural diseases. It has long been known that as a tree's growing area goes down in latitude, it goes up in elevation. Therefore, some native Canadian woods can be found growing naturally in the mountains of Georgia. Because of natural and purposeful hybridization, new forests plantings outside the original ranges produce vigorous trees, which in turn may cross with natural species. Therefore, wood in lumber yards today may be quite far removed from its cousins of the 18th century and before.

When trees were felled by hand, high mountainous areas were inaccessible to the hauling methods, and therefore these stands were ignored. The lower areas were sometimes overcut to provide the required lumber. Modern conservation and technology have combined today to utilize the entire forest evenly. While new techniques open the dangerous mountain areas to reasonable harvests, lower areas are managed properly to maintain wildlife cycles and ensure future tree crops.

Railroads began the job of opening up the forests, and today roads have been cut by bulldozers. Bulldozers can also build ledges into a hillside on which logs are stacked and moved. Huge tractors cut, haul and load logs at various stages of their progress through the forests to the mills.

Timber awaiting transport to a sawmill in Greece.

Overmature trees in Morocco.

Today, in much of the tropical hardwood forests as in the temperate zones, high powered harvesting machinery is replacing selective felling and hauling by elephant or oxen. Prime woods such as mahogany, padouk and teak are individually handled, while the less important trees of the forest are cut together and used for construction lumber, particleboard and paper pulp. In the place of these harvested trees, new fast-growing varieties will be planted. New plantations are replacing the old tropical forests. The true rain forests may eventually survive only as national parks and wildlife preserves.

Congo workers clear vines from the base of a tree.

Farmers clearing land in Liberia, 1963.

Trunks are sectioned before being transported for processing in the Congo.

A tractor does the work in the Congo.

Mahogany logs transported on the Ivory Coast.

These logs are loaded onto a train in the Congo which will take them to the port of Pointe-Noire.

Huge trunks of mahogany are floated down a river in the Ivory Coast.

Logs from the Congo are being loaded into the load of a ship.

Bulk ships are currently transporting lumber worldwide.

Hardwood lumber awaits many destinations.

A writer in *Forbes Magazine,* Oct. 15, 1977, reported that an estimated 6 billion board feet of United States National Forest Service timber is wasted every year to rot, insect and wind kill.

This would be enough to make the U.S. an exporter of lumber. It is the Congress that appropriates money for the Forest Service that is limiting the yield, not the foresters who work hard to properly manage the land.

Chapter 5   The Modern Wood Industry

The result of well-managed forests and mechanically developed transportation systems is a high yield of wood for thousands of final products. To sort out the best use for each wood, grading techniques have been developed.

The quality of wood directly affects its value. Boards that are free from knots, straight grained, and at least eight feet long are most valuable, and called first grade lumber. These are used for veneer making, paneling and best quality furniture construction. Boards that have occasional small knots are second grade, less valuable than first, and used for smaller lumber of interior construction. The poorest lumber, third grade, has numerous knot holes and uneven grain. This lumber can be used for plywood cores, particle board, or paper pulp. No wood needs to be wasted.

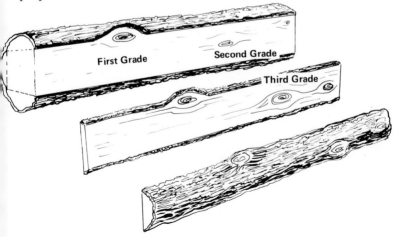

First Grade   Second Grade

Third Grade

Surface defects indicate grade

113

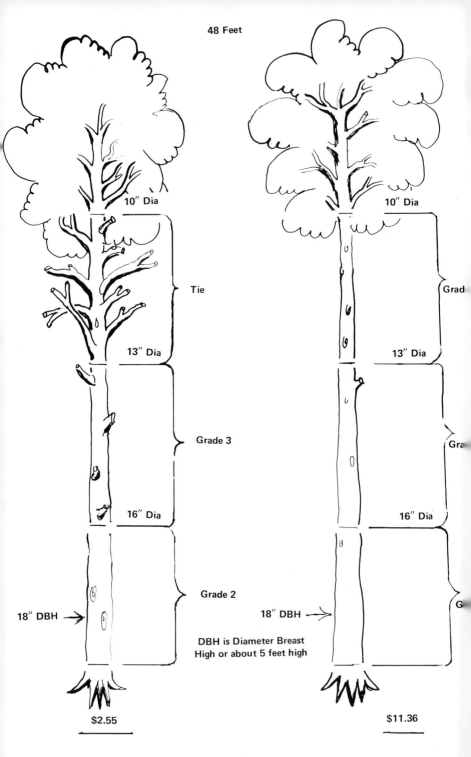

48 Feet

10" Dia

Tie

13" Dia

Grade 3

16" Dia

Grade 2

18" DBH →

DBH is Diameter Breast
High or about 5 feet high

$2.55

10" Dia

Grad

13" Dia

Gra

16" Dia

G

18" DBH →

$11.36

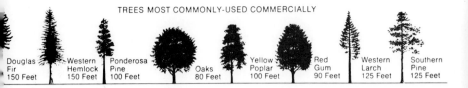

TREES MOST COMMONLY-USED COMMERCIALLY

| Douglas Fir 150 Feet | Western Hemlock 150 Feet | Ponderosa Pine 100 Feet | Oaks 80 Feet | Yellow Poplar 100 Feet | Red Gum 90 Feet | Western Larch 125 Feet | Southern Pine 125 Feet |

Particle board is made of layers of wood chips and adhesives. The size of the chips can be varied for different uses. For example, coarse chips in the center give strength while small chips on the outer edge give a smooth surface for veneer application. Stronger boards of coarse chips throughout have a rougher surface but more stability.

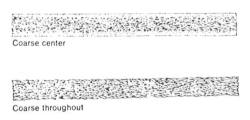

Coarse center

Coarse throughout

Irregular and small wood can be sent to pulp mills and processed for paper manufacturing. The growing use of paper products has prompted industries to develop specialized papers for particular uses. Papermaking is a major worldwide industry that is helping to develop national economies.

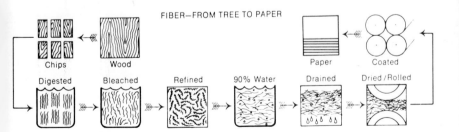

FIBER—FROM TREE TO PAPER

Chips — Wood — Paper — Coated

Digested — Bleached — Refined — 90% Water — Drained — Dried/Rolled

115

Kiln Drying of Lumber

Years ago, in order to get lumber dry enough for fine interior and cabinet work, the wood was stacked outdoors or in large barns for 7 to 10 years. Today, lumber is cut, then aged in a yard with strips of wood separating the boards to allow air ventilation. Lumber for kilning is grouped in units of 1,500–2,000 board feet. The lumber is usually aged a year for every inch of thickness. Moisture from dew and rain dries fast from the surface and does not affect the overall drying process. Most of the boards are painted red at the ends to prevent cracking during the aging process at the drying yard. Wood should go into the kiln with no more than 25% moisture content. Kiln drying gets the wood to a moisture content of 6–7½%. Air drying usually can do no better than 12–15% moisture content.

One inch thick lumber takes 21 days to fully dry, 2" lumber takes 45 days. Oak for industrial use is rarely kiln dried. If the wood is dried too quickly, moisture will explode, leaving disfigured wood cells called "honeycomb." This honeycomb can be just under the surface and not revealed until the boards are planed. Honeycombed wood is useless for cabinetry.

Since kilning is not a foolproof method of drying the wood, random boards are tested electronically during the kilning process to determine their moisture content. A test board is pulled out of the kiln each day and a piece cut off. This piece is weighed, burned and the residue weighed. From the difference in weight, the moisture content can be determined. If, by chance, an atypical board is chosen, the entire lot may be ruined. Kiln dried wood has very little chance for shrinkage as the wood is dried more than it could dry naturally.

Green lumber is stacked and ready to go into dry kilns.

Hardwood lumber is moved through the warehouses by modern, specialized machinery.

As the logging and processing of wood has changed over the decades, the uses of wood and wood products has changed too. Plywood has become standard building material because it is stronger and more durable than single boards. Particle board has found many uses in construction and paneling. Paper utilization has increased enormously as computer readouts run the world. Sawdust can be used for fuel in lumber yards, and as bedding for cattle and hogs. In Sweden, treated sawdust has been used as animal feed for many years.

One of the biggest changes in the building industry today has been that home builders who used to require enormous amounts of specialized millwork for window moldings, sashes and cornices, are now using metal and stock moldings whenever possible. The demands for custom mill work are now very limited. Kitchen cabinets and shop interiors are made of standard stock. Room baseboards were 8″ high 50 years ago, then became 6″ high, and are now down to 3–4″ high. The cost of these interior details has risen throughout the lumber industry, causing their present minimal use.

The old versus the new in methods of cutting lumber.

Puzzly desk made of solid ash in France. Yugoslavian slat chair made of beech.

Redwood furniture of contemporary design.

Chapter 6 Wood Descriptions

RED ASH

Fraxinus pennsylvanica

a hardwood

Also called "green ash," this is the most widely distributed of the ash group ranging throughout the middle Atlantic United States from lower New England to northern Florida, and west to the states just west of the Mississippi River.

The wood is hard, heavy, and coarse grained, weighing 41 lbs. per cubic foot at 12% moisture content. The heartwood is light brown with lighter sapwood that is often streaked with yellow, enabling it to be confused easily with the more valuable white ash. Ash is found in some of the American Pilgrim furniture of the late 17th and early 18th century. The tree grows best in moist, rich soil of the lowlands near water, and can grow to be 40 to 60 ft. high with a diameter of 18 to 20 inches.

This wood is not often found in modern lumber yards, but is made into wall paneling commercially.

WHITE ASH

Fraxinus americana

a hardwood

America's number one pastime owes a great deal of success to the wood of the white ash tree. After being cured for seven years, the best of this wood is made into Major League baseball bats. Because the tree grows rapidly in the spring, the summerwood is very strong, hard and dense, making it very tough. The impact of a hard ball and a forceful swing would crack most other woods, but white ash can send the ball out of the park. The wood has white to brown variations but not a clear color distinction of sapwood and heartwood. The straight grain is distinct between porous springwood and dense summerwood.

This is the largest and most common of the ashes, growing in the eastern United States to the piedmont regions of North and South Carolina and Georgia, and west to the Mississippi River, except Minnesota. It thrives in full sunlight and rich, fertile, moist soil near streams.

The tree grows to 80 feet high, with exceptional ones higher, and usually has a mature diameter of four to six feet, and a maximum age of about 200 years. Large pure woods of ash are rarely found today. The wood decays fairly rapidly when exposed to weather for extended periods. It weighs 41 lbs. per cubic foot.

This is a good wood for furniture since it is strong and hard, and can be worked well. The figure of the wood is attractive, and it takes a finish well.

Besides being made into baseball bats, ash is found in other sporting equipment including tennis rackets, snowshoes, polo sticks, hockey sticks, and boat oars. It makes wonderful tool handles, both the long straight variety and curved, as it is flexible enough to be shaped and stay strong.

Modern furniture makers use white ash for upholstery frames, while the better grades are used for exterior boards.

Wood sample #1 is white ash.

A white ash 22 feet around in Glen Mills, Pennsylvania.

BASSWOOD

Tilia americana

a hardwood

The American basswood is an abundant tree which grows in the northern part of the United States from Maine to West Virginia and west to Minnesota, Iowa and Missouri. It is the American linden or lime tree in some areas.

The tree stands tall and straight about 120 feet high and grows to about 4 feet in diameter when mature. The wood is uniformly pale yellow with little figure or differentiating between the heartwood and sapwood but with occasional mineral streaks. It is lightweight, only 26 lbs. per cubic foot, weak and soft, with significant shrinkage until it has dried, whereupon it becomes stable. The wood is easy to carve, and often favored among craftsmen who required sharp detail. The English master carver Grinling Gibbons working about 1670 to 1710, and his followers chose basswood for carving details in furniture and interior designs. The wood can also be ground and used for Japanned furniture and inlayed details. Because it is such a soft wood, it is rarely used outdoors. Besides wood carvings, basswood is useful as a molding material for picture frames, woodwork that will be painted, engineering patterns and hat and shoe blocks. Modern furniture manufacturers often use basswood for drawer backs because it is so light. Since the wood imparts no taste or odor to its contents, basswood is frequently chosen for food containers, crates and boxes

An interesting relationship exists between honey bees and basswood. The nectar of the basswood flower has a fragrance which is attractive to the honeybee, and the honey holds this fragrance. The basswood itself is the primary wood beekeepers choose for their hives since it is lightweight and easily worked with no harmful oils to affect the bees or honey.

BEECH

Fagus grandifolia

a hardwood

A beech tree in Tennessee bears the inscription: "D. Boon cillED A BAR On Tree in thE yEar 1760." All bear hunters recognize a bear's love of beech nuts.

The American beech has identifiable dark pores in conspicuous rays. It is hard, but brittle, used for flooring, not suitable for outdoor use. It is, however, bendable, remaining strong. The sapwood is white, deepening to red heartwood.

The tree stands up to 120 feet high and up to four feet in diameter. It weighs 44 lbs. per cubic foot. Beech grows naturally in the eastern United States from Maine to Florida and west to Michigan, Illinois and Alabama. The beech is found along mountain slopes and rich uplands in nearly pure forests, and along lower elevations further south.

This wood is very difficult to dry, with losses up to 30% during kilning. Because it can be highly polished and finished well, it is used where fancy grain is not desired. Drawer runners are often beech because they wear slick. The bending property lends it to use in bentwood furniture, box and basket construction. It does not take white lead or zinc oxide paints well. The wood does not give food flavor or color, so has been a suitable medium for utensils and containers for many years. European beech is notably found in English furniture, of the William and Mary period when it was painted, and in fancy painted furniture. Despite its strength, it decays rather easily.

Wood sample #2 is European beech.

128

BLACK BIRCH

Betula lenta

a hardwood

   This is equally well known as sweet birch, and the origin of the sweet sap for birch beer. The tree lives along the Appalachian and Allegheny Mountain chain from southern Maine to Georgia in rich soil. The black and yellow birch woods are used interchangeably commercially for chemicals and millwork, usually not being differentiated. The heartwood is reddish-brown and sapwood whitish, both hard, heavy, and close grained. Black birch can be highly polished into a beautiful finish. It weighs 44 lbs. per cubic foot.

RED BIRCH

Betula nigra

a hardwood

   The red birch is also known as the river birch and thrives in deep rich soil of swamps, and streams from Massachusetts, along the eastern seaboard to Northern Florida and west in low areas to Eastern Texas. It can grow to heights of about 80 feet and diameters of three feet. The wood is light or medium tan with pale sapwood. When it is not stained cherry or mahogany red, it looks bland and muddy, especially in the sapwood areas. The red birch has less figure than the other types of birch listed here. Weighing 37 lbs. per cubic foot, this birch is strong and has a high shock resistance. It is a good wood for turning and shaping, but holds nails only fairly well. Birch is found in some early colonial American furniture, especially in Windsor styles. As a veneer it is sometimes found on furniture of the late 18th century. Curly burled examples are found.

   Today red birch is used as a core for plywood, in moldings, door jambs and cabinet work because it is strong. It is more expensive than tulip poplar, but less expensive than white pine. It takes high quality woodworking tools to work with it, but the durability is usually worth the effort.

When looking at a piece of red birch, it can be compared with ash, but has finer and fainter dark pores. With these fine lines the wood has been stained to resemble walnut, maple and cherry on both antique and modern furniture. Many woods originally thought to be something else have turned out to be birch under microscopic examination.

A birchwood clogging camp, 1910, showing the pyramids of the roughly cut c soles and the cloggers with their stock-knives standing by.

WHITE BIRCH

Betula papyrifera

a hardwood

This is the paper birch or canoe birch whose easily peeled white bark the American Indians used to build their canoes. The tree grows in northern New England, northern Michigan and Wisconsin, with spotty areas in the mountains of New York and Pennsylvania. The tree is usually slim, up to 80 feet high, about two feet in diameter and growing in clumps of two to four together. The wood is hard, strong and close grained weighing 44 lbs. per cubic foot. Today veneers, spools and bobbins, and pulpwood are common products; and in the state of Maine, toothpicks from white birch are made in a large-scale industry. The lumber of the white and red birches is combined for commercial use without distinction one from the other.

YELLOW BIRCH

Betula alleghaniensis

a hardwood

This is the most common commercial American birch named for its yellowish-bronze bark that peels in long horizontal strips. Yellow birch grows in the northeastern United States, Great Lakes states, and above 3,000 feet elevation in the Appalachian Mountains. It is usually found on hilly terrain. The wood is heavy, hard, strong and stiff with a low decay resistance. It is best worked with machines rather than hand tools, and takes a high polish. Today, yellow birch lumber is made into furniture, wooden dishes, handles, interior finish and doors. This wood takes a walnut stain well. It weighs 44 lbs. per cubic foot. The veneers go into baskets, boxes, plywood and airplane construction.

From the wood distillates are made into wood alcohol, also acetate of lime, charcoal, tar and oils are produced for industrial use. Yellow birch is mixed with hard maples and used for pulpwood.

Wood sample #3 is Yellow Birch.

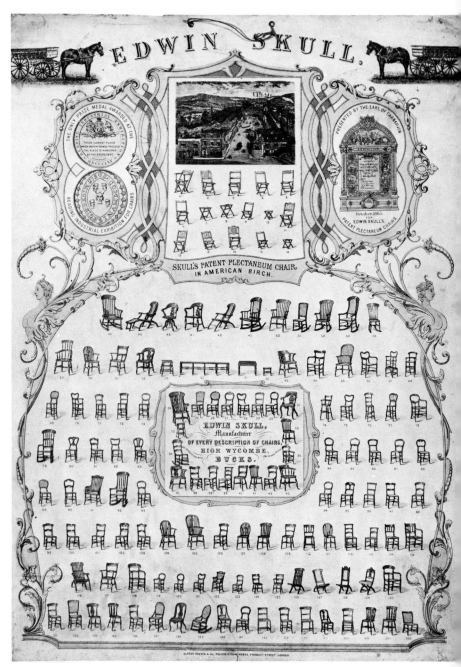

Edwin Skull's broadsheet of chair designs shows 142 chairs that were available about 1865 made of American birch.

BUTTERNUT

Juglans cinerea

a hardwood

Butternut, in the walnut family and sometimes referred to as white walnut, is a softer wood than black walnut. It is not a common tree in any area, but grows well in rich, moist soil of rocky hills and stream banks from Maine to Delaware and eastern Virginia, and westward into eastern Iowa and Missouri. It does not grow in coastal regions.

The butternut tree is usually 40 to 60 feet high, sometimes up to 100 feet high, with a trunk 2 to 3 feet in diameter. The wood is fairly soft, with tan or pinkish-brown heartwood streaked with red or yellow, and white or light brown sapwood that darkens with exposure. The wood weighs 27 lbs. per cubic foot, and is resistant to decay. It saws beautifully, carves like butter, glues very well, and can be worked with hand tools, but slim turnings will break. It takes all stains well and finishes beautifully.

In American furniture, butternut was used in the eighteenth century, and with stains, into the Victorian period. When butternut is cut into, a white surface will show regardless of the stain, whereas when true walnut is cut into, the surface is purple. Today, not much butternut is cut. Since it is usually a by-product of hardwood lumber operations, the industry does not have figures on its yield, but probably no more than a million board feet is cut in a year. Some lumber is made into veneers. The American colonists could make a yellow-orange dye from the green husks of the butternut fruit.

Butternut has not been used extensively for furniture for many years. In the 18th century it was used quite widely. Today, very few specialty lumber yards stock butternut—and one owner told me he has had this lot for 10 years.

EASTERN RED CEDAR

Juniperus virginiana

a softwood

A sweet-tasting, aromatic oil in the eastern red cedar wood distinguishes this tree from all others. The knottier the wood, the stronger the scent. Moth larvae, those hole-making nuisances that can spoil clothes, are killed by this scent, while man seems to enjoy it. Therefore, the wood is a favorite lining material for storage chests and closets. The oil also makes the wood watertight.

Eastern red cedar wood is close grained and brittle, with dark red heartwood and white sapwood that darkens to tan with exposure. The wood is straight grained, easy to work, and resists decay for long periods. The wood comes from trees that grow as small bushes or sometimes up to 90 feet high and three feet in diameter. They prefer dry, gravelly slopes and limestone hills, and range from southern Nova Scotia to Georgia along the coast and west to the Mississippi River states, and in the West Indies.

The lumber is well suited for fence posts, and building sills. Three-quarter inch knotty boards make the best mothproof-furniture linings, and the water resistant properties qualify the wood for use in greenhouses for small buckets where strength is not a requirement. The wood also makes handsome, water resistant boat decks.

Evelyn records the importation of red cedar into England in the 18th century where it turns up as linings for small, then larger drawers, and occasionally as a primary wood in furniture. Bermuda 18th century furniture is sometimes identified by the use of cedar in styles made by Philadelphia cabinetmakers who sailed with the merchant ships to Bermuda.

Wood sample #4 is eastern red cedar.

This slipper chair was made in Bermuda in the eighteenth century of cedar and cherry wood. Cabinetmakers from Philadelphia traveled to Bermuda in merchants' ships. Therefore, the style is comparable to that found in the Philadelphia area but with a Bermuda interpretation. The knees resemble the style of William Savery, and the trifid feet are common in the valley of the Delaware River.

NORTHERN WHITE CEDAR
Thuja occidentalis

a softwood

   This is the arborvitae or Tree of Life that is popular as an ornamental planting. Northern white cedar grows in the northeastern United States and southeastern Canada to southern New Hampshire, central Massachusetts, New York and west to Minnesota, with areas in high mountains of Virginia, West Virginia and Tennessee. It has been growing also in Europe since the middle of the sixteenth century. The tree stands 50 to 60 feet high, usually 2 to 3 feet in diameter with exceptions to six feet. Often two or three secondary stems branch from the low main trunk. The wood is pale yellow-brown with a light fragrance. It is very coarse grained, but soft and durable. This, as well as the other cedars, is well suited for fence posts, shingles and railway ties as the oils make it resistant to decay. Medicine making uses some of the oil extracts.

SOUTHERN WHITE CEDAR

Chamaecyparis thyoides

a softwood

This cedar grows along streams and at the edges of fresh-water swamps. The natural oils protect it from decay and water-soaking even when the wood is submerged for long periods of time. It grows in pockets from New Jersey to Florida and the Gulf Coast to Louisiana. Virginia's Dismal Swamp produces a large quantity of this southern white cedar. The trees stand 60 to 80 feet high and 3 feet in diameter. The wood is lightweight and easily worked but not strong. The heartwood is light brown with red or pink tones and lighter sapwood.

This is a favoriate material for boat work and canoe construction, as well as fences and shingles. Logs that have been submerged for centuries have been found in perfect condition in southern New Jersey swamplands.

Furniture made in Philadelphia at the end of the eighteenth century often has this white cedar wood as drawer bottoms. It was apparently readily available from the New Jersey lowlands.

CEDRO

Cedrela

a hardwood

Cedro is a cousin of the mahogany group and is commercially known as Spanish cedar. The seven species grow in Mexico, the West Indies, and all the Latin American countries except Chile. The most important and widespread are *Cedrela odorata, Cedrela angustifolia,* and *Cedrela fissilis.* The heartwood is pinkish-red or brown darkening with exposure.

136

There is an odor like cedar, and the wood has a coarser texture than mahogany. It weighs 26 lbs. per cubic foot—much lighter than any of the true mahoganies. Cedro contains an aromatic oil which can corrode metal mechanisms housed inside, so its use for clocks and instrument cases is not recommended. The wood is decay resistant when hard, but the sapwood is attacked by powder-post beetles. The wood cuts well because it is so soft. It can be made into cabinets, patterns, and musical instruments.

It cannot be determined today if North American wood inventories of the mid-eighteenth century that list "cedar" and "red cedar" actually refer to Spanish cedar or the native red cedar, for it is possible that both were available to port cities.

BLACK CHERRY

Prunus serotina
a hardwood

Of the many cherry trees that grow in the United States, only the black cherry is commercially valuable. It grows in scattered areas from Maine to Florida and west to the Mississippi River. The tree is usually small, up to 60 or 80 feet high and two to three feet in diameter. It grows in rich moist soil of the Appalachian mountain range; its largest trees on the Allegheny Mountains from West Virginia to Georgia. In New England it will grow on cliffs above the ocean.

The wood is heavy and strong, reddish brown with a speckled pattern that can be stained pink to brown and finished to a beautiful sheen. Fancy grains can be found in notches and burls. It weighs 35 lbs. per cubic foot. Black cherry wood is particularly stable once dry, without a tendency to warp. Therefore, it is perfectly suited for mounting plates to be engraved and is used by the best engravers who require exact reproductions. For example, a dollar bill is engraved with cherry wood in the process.

Cherry furniture has been admired for generations, especially in New England where the wood used to be plentiful. Wide boards are most uncommon as the width of the trees is usually limited. Today cherry veneer is in popular decorative

137

use over softer wood cases, and solid cherry is used in very expensive furniture.

An extract from the bark of the black cherry tree is used in medicine as a sedative or tonic. The fruit can be used to flavor rum and brandy.

Wood sample #5 is black cherry.

Connecticut cherry furniture, such as this wonderful highboy, retains a deep, rich brown color when it hasn't been refinished. The carved drawer exemplifies the restraint Connecticut makers of the eighteenth century used in decorating their furniture.

CHESTNUT
Castanea dentata
a hardwood

A cargo of Japanese chestnut fruit that landed at Albany, New York in 1907, contained a disease which killed practically every American chestnut tree. Now entirely harvested, the wood, which was not affected by the blight, is available in some lumber yards. Some damage, however, has resulted at the yards by wood-boring worms that attack dead wood. Therefore, much of the wood is especially desirable because of its unusual appearance and is used for picture frames. Chestnut is also a principal ingredient in tanning lumber as the tannin is extracted and used to dye animal hides.

The chestnut tree grew in North America from southern Maine to Delaware and Ohio and southern Illinois, and at altitudes of 4,000 feet along the Appalachian Mountains to Georgia and western Florida. The tree could grow to 100 feet and 3 to 4 feet in diameter and larger. The wood is light and soft and apt to warp while drying. Light grey-brown in color, it has tiny dark lines that appear to be etched. This wood weighs 30 lbs. per cubic foot.

The chestnuts were collected in the last century and sold roasted in larger towns.

The wood was frequently used as a secondary wood in Rhode Island and Pennsylvania in the 18th century. It looks very much like oak, but does not have the rays. It is used in Windsor chairs.

There were still many tall dead chestnut trees standing in the woods of Pennsylvania in 1938.

CYPRESS
Taxodium distichum
a softwood

The construction crews digging the foundations of the Mayflower Hotel in downtown Washington, D.C. uncovered cypress logs that proved to be at least 100,000 years old. These trees thrive in water, preferring to be submerged at least part of the year. A natural resin preserves the wood and makes it especially suitable for outdoor use. The tree often has a buttressed base with "knees" that supply air to the roots. The trunk rises and tapers, sometimes becoming hollow and enlarged, and reaches a height of about 150 feet and up to 12 feet in diameter. They are confined to coastal swamps from southern New Jersey and Delaware to southern Florida and the Gulf States. Quite often they are weird supporters of Spanish moss. The wood is light and not strong, but very durable, especially the heartwood. It can vary in color from light brown to nearly black; the darker the color, the more durable the wood. It is well suited for use in outdoor construction, posts and fences, cooperage, docks, bridges, greenhouses, water towers, tanks, boats and river pilings.

A variety of cypress has infrequently turned up as secondary wood in furniture made in Charleston, S.C. in the 18th century.

Wood sample #6 is cypress from Florida.

EBONY

Diospyros
a hardwood

When a furniture-minded individual thinks of ebony, he sees a jet-black wood used to decorate ornate furniture. This ebony is probably *Diospyros ebenum* of Ceylon. The color of most species varies from African *Diospyros crassiflora*'s jet black, through 200 African and East Indian species that are non-uniform, variegated shades of grayish-white, reddish-gray and brownish-gray.

Wood sample #7 is an ebony from Macassar, India.

Generally, ebony trees stand about 70 feet high and up to 30 inches in diameter, but the darker woods are found in small trees of particular species, in very small quantity. The sapwood is white. The wood is heavy and close grained with little figure, except the color variations. The wood is very likely to split in large pieces, and must be dried slowly. Therefore, it is best kept covered and shipped in small pieces. This

140

dense wood will dull almost all woodworking equipment, and can best be worked with metalworking tools. It finishes smooth and can be highly polished. Because of the difficulty handling it, it is a very costly wood.

Ebony is found on musical instruments and fancy furniture of the eighteenth, nineteenth and twentieth centuries.

Historically, ebony has its place in circles of fashion. The show of treasures from Tutankamon's tomb includes an ebony chair, jet black with decorative additions. In the 17th century in England, Catherine of Breganza brought 2 chairs with her from Goa for her marriage to King Charles I. These created an upheaval in contemporary taste, like the first Lear jets of recent years. They became a sign of culture and status. Therefore, almost all the owners of cane-backed chairs in England painted the wood black to resemble ebony. The taste soon came to America. A set of maple Queen Anne chairs, labeled and made in Philadelphia by William Savery in the mid-eighteenth century retain their original black paint. These were recently sold to the William Penn Memorial Museum in Harrisburg, Penna.

In the last years of the eighteenth and early nineteenth century ebony appeared on furniture as leg cuffs, line stringing and as contrast to light woods.

Today, solid black woods are usually stained, not natural.

WHITE ELM

Ulums americana
a hardwood

The white elm tree grows in low, rich hilly soil such as the banks of streams abundantly in the northern east and midwest United States, and gradually less abundantly further south. It is a straight, uniform tree favored for ornamental planting throughout its range. There is one at Berkeley Springs, West Virginia which now has a diameter of about seven feet that George Washington planted at the intersection of the main streets while working as a surveyor for Lord Fairfax. The tree usually grows 60 to 80 feet high and 6 to 11 feet in diameter. The white elm wood is heavy, 35 lbs. per cubic foot, strong, difficult to split, and easy to bend. It is cream or light brown with coarse texture, a straight grain and high shock resistance. It is difficult to work with hand tools, but holds nails and screws well.

Elm is found in bent parts of furniture, especially chairs, sometimes requiring steaming to hold the form. These flexible tendencies make elm suitable for barrel staves and the tendency not to split makes it useful as wagon wheel hubs.

Commercially today elm at the lumber yard may be white elm, or any of the five other elms that grow in the United States: hard rock elm, winged elm, slippery elm, cedar elm, or rarely from the south, red elm. Close cousins are the English elm and Scottish elm that are frequently found on antique British Windsor chairs.

Wood sample #8 is white elm.

To illustrate burls which can appear in many hardwoods, wood sample # 9 is included. This is an elm burl from the Carpathian Mountain region.

DOUGLAS FIR

Pseudotsuga taxifolia
a softwood

Douglas fir is a primary lumber producer in the western United States, and is called many other names locally, including Douglas spruce, fir, yellow fir, red pine, red spruce, red fir, and Oregon pine. Confusion can ensue when speaking of this wood unless the Latin name is used.

Douglas fir is a rapidly growing, straight, tall tree usually 200 feet tall on the coast and 100 feet tall inland, and can vary between three and twelve feet in diameter. It grows along the Pacific coast from British Columbia along the Rocky Mountains into Mexico, a range 2,000 miles long and 1,000 miles wide.

The wood quality varies depending on the growth conditions, but is generally strong for its weight, and medium hard with a grainy, knotty texture. The color can vary from pinkish yellow to reddish brown. These properties suit many

142

forms of construction needs including building interiors such as doors, sashes, trim and flooring. Plywood is probably the most frequent use of Douglas fir wood, but it is also used for railway ties, fuel, and ladders. The sheer volume of Douglas fir wood produced is permitted by the very large size of the tree.

With their ten-foot cross-cut saw and axes in hand, these men felled Douglas fir about 1900.

A forester inspects a stand of young Douglas fir.

RED GUM

Liquidambar styraciflua

a hardwood

Red gum is the leading wood for interior furniture construction today, and sometimes goes by the name sweet gum. The tree grows to 140 feet high and can be five feet in diameter. It weighs 34 lbs. per cubic foot. Gum grows from coastal Connecticut to southeastern Pennsylvania and south to central Florida, southwest through Kentucky, Tennessee, and Arkansas to eastern Texas. It does not grow at high altitudes, preferring low borders of swamps. The wood can be plane or figured of yellow or red toned heartwood and pale red or nearly white sapwood. This wood can warp, but cuts well at any angle. It appears in antique case furniture of New Jersey and the Delaware river valley where it is a local wood. New Jersey linen presses and Hudson river valley schranks are particularly noteworthy. The Henry Francis du Pont

Winterthur Museum has a Hudson River Valley highboy of gumwood. Because it takes any stain well, it can be made to look like walnut, cherry, or maple.

Besides furniture, it is used commercially today for paneling, doors, interior trim, dishes, fruit boxes and excelsior.

Wood sample #10 is red gum from the Carolinas.

HICKORY

Carya

a hardwood

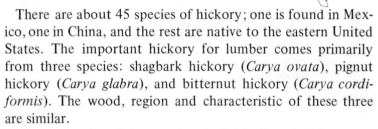

There are about 45 species of hickory; one is found in Mexico, one in China, and the rest are native to the eastern United States. The important hickory for lumber comes primarily from three species: shagbark hickory (*Carya ovata*), pignut hickory (*Carya glabra*), and bitternut hickory (*Carya cordiformis*). The wood, region and characteristic of these three are similar.

The properties of the wood make it ideally suited for many uses. The wood is tough, resilient, quite hard, and weighs 51 lbs. per cubic foot. The sapwood is light cream colored while the heartwood can vary from light brown to reddish brown. Some woods are stronger, and some harder, but the combination in hickory is not found in any other wood. Therefore, the wood makes excellent tool handles, baskets, carriages, wagons and fuel. Harness racing developed in the United States with the invention of the light sulky in which hickory is a primary component. Hickory burns with an aromatic scent when green, and leaves a hot bed of coals over which meat can be smoked. The wood is second to ash for baseball bats. The trees can grow to 140 feet high and 4 feet in diameter in wet woods that border streams and rolling uplands. The three hickories for lumber range from southern Maine to northwestern Florida, and out to the midwest. The wood is susceptible to decay by insects, and once cut by borers.

Commercially today the wood is sometimes substituted for chestnut because the two are so similar. Hickory can also be confused with ash and oak, but hickory has shorter, tighter and more uniform pores that resemble etched lines. These are also translucent medullary rays nearly parallel to the "etched" pores. Oak has the medullary rays nearly perpendicular to the "etched" ones. In American antiques, hickory is found as Windsor chair spokes when strength is essential.

HOLLY

Ilex opaca

a hardwood

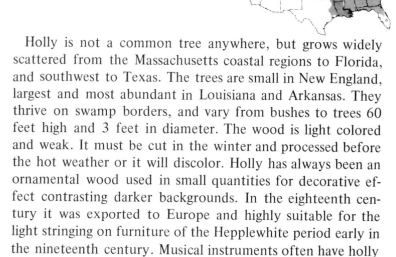

Holly is not a common tree anywhere, but grows widely scattered from the Massachusetts coastal regions to Florida, and southwest to Texas. The trees are small in New England, largest and most abundant in Louisiana and Arkansas. They thrive on swamp borders, and vary from bushes to trees 60 feet high and 3 feet in diameter. The wood is light colored and weak. It must be cut in the winter and processed before the hot weather or it will discolor. Holly has always been an ornamental wood used in small quantities for decorative effect contrasting darker backgrounds. In the eighteenth century it was exported to Europe and highly suitable for the light stringing on furniture of the Hepplewhite period early in the nineteenth century. Musical instruments often have holly inlay. By placing an inlay in hot sand, edges can be burned and shaded to dark tones. Much of the decorative inlay is varied this way.

Furniture peculiar to Chester County, Pennsylvania has holly inlay in a ball and berry pattern on eighteenth century chests, clocks, boxes and desks.

Holly is not available in lumber yards today.

Wood sample #11 is holly from Indiana.

LIGNUM VITAE

Guaicum officinale

a hardwood

Growing only in the West Indies and sparsely in the American tropical mainland, lignum vitae is an exotic wood that was used in the eighteenth century for furniture in Holland and the British Isles. The tree is usually short and crooked, only about thirty feet high and a foot in diameter at maturity. Old shipping records include remarks about logs 20 inches in diameter from Cuba and Santo Domingo. The sapwood is yellow and makes up half the trunk, with greenish or blackish streaks on the brown heartwood. This is the heaviest and hardest wood known with a density like iron. The grain is fine and uniform with unusual alternating spirals that account for its great strength. When first cut, the wood has an oil with a pleasant scent and bitter taste, and the soft wood can be worked easily. However, as the wood dries, it becomes rock hard and oily. Besides its ornamental uses on furniture, it is well suited for machinery where lubrication is impractical such as underwater bearings. It is found as handles for ladles, being tougher than ebony.

AFRICAN MAHOGANY

Khaya ivorensis and *Khaya senegalensis*

a hardwood

African mahogany was exported to England in 1830 where it was considered more inferior than the West Indian mahoganies the English were using. Nevertheless, large exports continued to other parts of the world where it has been used extensively in cabinet work. *Khaya ivorensis* grows in Nigeria, and along the Ivory and Gold Coasts. *Khaya senegalensis* is distributed there and other areas of West Africa. The tree stands up to 150 feet high and 8 to 10 feet in diameter. Today, average logs are 35 feet long and 5 feet in diameter. This wood varies in color from light to reddish brown, frequently with figures that are more pronounced than Honduran mahogany. There are also larger pores and a milder texture than the other mahoganies. It is a heavy wood, averaging 35 lbs. per cubic foot. These trees grow individually, one to 6 or 8 acres.

When harvested, the sapwood is often removed to prevent ambrosia beetles from causing pin-sized holes. Since it is such a heavy wood, it is often squared in the forest before being transported to a mill.

Today, large quantities are available and used for furniture, boatbuilding and high quality plywood.

African mahogany at the Ivory Coast.

HONDURAS MAHOGANY

Swietenia macrophylla

a hardwood

In 1886, Honduras or Central American mahogany was differentiated from the West Indian varieties. This species grows in Central America, Colombia, Venezuela, upper Amazon River in Peru, Bolovia and Brazil. However, there is no distinction between the varieties for export. All the lumber is called Honduras mahogany commercially. The tree grows in damp ground with wood variations directly affected by the conditions, soil and wind. It frequently stands over 100 feet high and may measure 40 feet around. The best lumber is obtained from above a large buttress which can go 15 feet up the trunk. The wood averages 32 lbs. per cubic foot, but can be as heavy as 48 lbs. The trees grow scattered, about 1 to every 2 or 3 acres. The first trees to be cut were from the coast, then along the waterways by which they could be moved. Inland trees stood unharvested for many years until need made them practical to move. When first cut the sapwood is colorless, and heartwood bright pink fading to a dark rich copper-red shade with exposure to sunlight. The faint grain has sometimes shown exciting figures especially in the wood cut in the early 19th century. The wood cuts well and is often carved, with very little shrinkage or warping. Therefore, this is a leading furniture wood.

Wood samples # 12 and 13 are Honduras mahogany shown plain and striped.

PHILIPPINE MAHOGANY

Shorea

a hardwood

Philippine mahogany is a loose term combining the 4 main groups locally called Lauan including *Shorea almon, Shorea negrosensis, Shorea polysperma,* and *Shorea squamata.* They range from light to dark red in color. All the lumber from this group is shipped together. Although of coarser texture and softer than African or Honduras mahogany, Philippine is actually about as strong. It grows in the Philippine Islands and is quite easily kiln dried.

This low grade variety of the mahogany group is primarily used today for interior trim, low grade furniture, paneling, and boat construction.

Forestry trainees inspect a log of Philippine mahogany.

WEST INDIAN MAHOGANY

Swietenia mahogoni

a hardwood

Although not commercially available today, this group of wood was the primary mahogany of American furniture in the 18th century. The U.S. government literature has stated that "if the place of origin (of mahogany) is not known, it cannot be determined from examinations of the wood." So overlapping are the characteristics of mahogany from distant areas that no simple distinction can be given. Growing conditions, soil, exposure and finishing techniques contribute to variations in the figure.

The history of the import of mahogany from the West Indian Islands reads like a commercial chronology of world powers. The islands were owned variously by Spain and England: Santo Domingo, Puerto Rico, and Cuba by Spain;

Jamaica, the Bahamas, and Trinidad by England. Generally, Santo Domingo had the hardest wood, growing very slowly to great heights over 150 feet, and a weight of 50 lbs. per cubic foot. Cuban mahogany is next in weight, 40 lbs. per cubic foot. The other woods rank around and below these, depending on conditions.

The Spanish must have known of mahogany first, for it is found in woodwork and furniture built for the Escorial from 1563 to 1584. This is a full century before the English built Nottingham Castle with mahogany woodwork in 1680. Between the Christmases of 1699 and 1700, British import records list 36 pieces of Jamaican mahogany at £5. Some time prior to 1708, Philadelphia cabinetmaker, Charles Plumley, had 2 mahogany planks, and in 1710 William Till of Philadelphia had a very long mahogany board.* Before 1722 John Dickinson, merchant between Philadelphia and the West Indies, had mahogany furniture in his home. Walnut, though, was still the more common wood in that city. In 1748 notice was given in America that Jamaican mahogany was almost all cut down, yet imports were available for many years to come. The Federal styles took advantage of the fancy grains of solid and veneered mahogany, and in the early 1800's, Duncan Phyfe made constant use of these exotic figures. Records indicate that Santo Domingan mahogany was exported in increasing quantities to England between 1801 and 1841.

SILVER MAPLE

Acer saccharinum

a hardwood

Silver maple represents the soft maples which have more limited use than the hard maples. The wood of the silver maple is relatively lightweight and easily worked, but strong, close grained and somewhat brittle. It is sometimes difficult to distinguish the soft and hard maples, yet the wood of the soft is lighter colored throughout, and sometimes streaked with dark pith flecks that seldom appear in hard maple. The

*Hornor, William MacPherson, Jr., Blue Book, Philadelphia furniture, Philadelphia, 1935, p. 14.

Most Philadelphia carved chairs of this quality are mahogany, but walnut ones exist occasionally, a few are cherry, and one in every thousand is maple.

The Shaker furniture has classically simple lines that are distinctive. This chair is made of maple.

wood stains well and can be made to resemble several of the other hardwoods, especially fruitwoods. Silver maple trees prefer to grow in the sandy banks of streams, and occasionally in swampland. They range away from the coasts from Maine, through the Carolinas and west to the Mississippi River states, excluding Louisiana. Their best development is in the lower Ohio and Mississippi River valleys. The tree grows up to 120 feet high with a weight of 38 lbs. per cubic foot. Soft maple is used extensively for furniture, both solid and veneered, carved and plain; also for childrens' vehicles, and tool parts. This maple makes a good charcoal.

SUGAR MAPLE

Acer saccharum
a hardwood

Sugar maple represents the versatile hard maples used in solid and veneer forms as the all-purpose hardwood. The yield per year is enormous, and this wood has the most numerous applications.

The tree stands 75 to 100 feet high and 3 to 4 feet in diameter. It grows in the New England, northern midwestern and Great Lakes states. Its leaves give the autumn landscape brilliant reds, oranges and yellows—so the trees' value for ornamental uses cannot be ignored. The wood is light tan at the heartwood with white sapwood. It is strong, heavy, stiff and resilient, with a weight of 44 lbs. per cubic foot. Like the soft maples, the hard maples take stains well and polishes smooth and firm. The wood can be found straight grained or in curly, wavy, or birds' eye figures that are very desirable aesthetically. The figured veneers and solid boards appear in all manner of furniture where large panels can show off the grain. This wood turns well and is resistant to wear. Therefore, New England's colonists found it perfectly suited for turned elements of William and Mary furniture, and inside upholstered chairs and sofas.

This is also the tree from which sweet maple syrup and sugar is taken in the late winter as the sap rises. It is astound-

Striped maple is an exciting wood which is quite popular for furniture. This secretary has a rippling surface, yet is quite simple in design. It was made for the Wentworth family of Massachusetts. There has been an attempt made here to show depth by using wood of more contrasting stripe in the panels than on the stiles.

This Pennsylvania Windsor side chair is of superb proportion and has striped maple legs.

ing to think that a tree can produce 12 gallons of sap a year, and it takes 35 to 40 gallons of sap to make a gallon of pure syrup.

Wood sample # 14 is plain rock maple from New York and #15 is birds' eye figured maple.

RED OAK

Quercus rubra

a hardwood

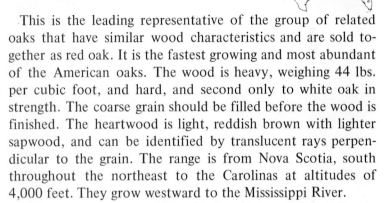

This is the leading representative of the group of related oaks that have similar wood characteristics and are sold together as red oak. It is the fastest growing and most abundant of the American oaks. The wood is heavy, weighing 44 lbs. per cubic foot, and hard, and second only to white oak in strength. The coarse grain should be filled before the wood is finished. The heartwood is light, reddish brown with lighter sapwood, and can be identified by translucent rays perpendicular to the grain. The range is from Nova Scotia, south throughout the northeast to the Carolinas at altitudes of 4,000 feet. They grow westward to the Mississippi River.

The tree is mature at 60 to 70 feet high and 2 to 3 feet in diameter, often with a short trunk and many branches. This is a hard wood that can be worked well and takes a good finish.

Red oak is used in all types of construction, flooring, boats, ladder rungs, nonwaterproof barrels, and can be heated easily with creosote to preserve it for use as railroad ties.

Furniture of most forms has been made of oak, but because of the excessive weight, lighter woods are used in non-structural areas of furniture today. It is interesting that now this wood is being exported to France, England and Germany which have found the civil unrest in Africa detrimental to their former suppliers.

The term "wainscot" is derived from Wagenschot, the word for oak boards used in interior wall finishing.

Red oak is the State tree of New Jersey.

Wood sample #16 is red oak.

WHITE OAK

Quercus alba

a hardwood

White oak is a commercial group of oak as well as a particular variety. Many of the characteristics are shared by the members of the group, making this one of the most important and abundant American woods. The white oak tree grows to 80 or 100 feet high at maturity with a trunk 3 to 4 feet in diameter. The growing conditions cause a wide ranging variety in the wood. If grown in a dense forest, the tree will be tall, if in the open, short. On high, well drained land, the wood will be of fine texture with even grain that is easy to work and less apt to swell. On low humid land, the oak is tough grained and hard. The sapwood and heartwood are both light brown, and the wood weighs 47 lbs. per cubic foot.

White oak grows in the eastern states from southern Maine across lower New England to the Florida border and west to the Mississippi River. It can tolerate a variety of conditions, flourishing on sandy plains, gravelly ridges, rich uplands and moist bottomlands, sometimes forming nearly pure forests.

The most durable wood flooring is made of white oak, this being harder and stronger than even red oak with a lighter and more uniform finish. It is used extensively in ship building, the making of agricultural tools, baskets, cabinetmaking, railway ties, fences and fuel. Natural tylose makes the wood waterproof and ideal for storing liquids, therefore for barrels and buckets.

Today white oak is exported to Europe in large quantities. It is the state tree of Maryland and Connecticut.

PADOUK

Pterocarpus dalbergioides

a hardwood

Andaman padouk, or vermilion wood, is a beautiful, exotic wood of purple or bright crimson under chocolate brown figure, more variable than the closely related Burmese padouk.

The English oak in this bird cage base is a strongly figured example of oak grain. Quarter sawn oak shows more rays and more interesting grain than tangential cuts. Notice the medullary ray here which cannot be seen in chestnut, hickory or ash.

This wood is heavy and strong, weighing 45 to 55 lbs. per cubic foot, easier to work but not quite as strong as Burmese. This variety grows only on the Andaman Islands in the Indian Ocean between Malaya and India on the banks of creeks. The tree stands up to a hundred feet high and eight feet in diameter. The tree's growing habits are reflected in the wood. Clear annual rings are recorded since the tree stands leafless for two months a year.

Padouk is favored for parquet floors, paneling, furniture, ship fittings, railings, and even billiard tables of high quality. At one time the wood was harvested by convict labor sent by the English from India and Burma.

It is used today in the Far East and China for furniture construction.

Wood sample #17 is Andaman padouk.

157

Clear white oak logs await the veneer saw.

PEAR

Pyrus communis

a hardwood

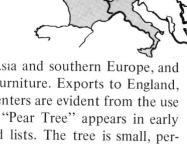

The pear tree originated in Asia and southern Europe, and is found primarily in French furniture. Exports to England, America and other furniture centers are evident from the use of pear in marquetry designs. "Pear Tree" appears in early American cabinetmakers' wood lists. The tree is small, perhaps reaching 50 feet high and eight feet in diameter at maturity. It grows in Germany, Switzerland, Italy, France and the United States, and is primarily cultivated for its fruit.

The wood is uniform, smooth, weighs 45 to 50 lbs. per cubic inch and carves beautifully. The sapwood is pale yellow and the heartwood rosy to red with light cream shadings. This wood is used for flesh tones in decorative inlay work.

French furniture of the 16th and 17th centuries often has pear wood if made in a region where it was available, and from the 18th century on, inlays of pear are found in distant areas. Perry, an alcoholic drink, is made from the fermented fruit.

158

LONGLEAF PINE

Pinus palustris

a softwood

This is the southern pine from which turpentine and rosin are made. As its name indicates, the needles are the longest of the pine group. The wood is very valuable because it is the heaviest, hardest, and strongest pine, being one of the hard pines of eastern forests.

The tree grows along the eastern coast of North and South Carolina, Georgia and Florida, the Gulf Coast of Alabama and Mississippi, and into western Louisiana and eastern Texas, preferring sandy or gravelly soil. The longleaf pine tree grows 100 to 120 feet high and up to three feet in diameter.

The heartwood is light red to orange, and the sapwood nearly white making a vivid contrast of light and dark stripes across the sawed surface. The grain is coarse, tough, durable, and resistant to decay. The sap is distilled into turpentine, with the residue becoming resin for the baseball pitcher and boxing ring. The wood is made into ship masts and spars, bridges, viaducts, flooring, charcoal and pulpwood.

Another variety, the slash pine (*Pinus elliottii*), grows in the southern region of the longleaf range and has very similar wood. Therefore, these woods are shipped together as longleaf pine in commercial trade today.

PINE SUGAR

Pinus lambertiana

a softwood

Sugar pine is a hard pine that grows in the Cascade Mountains of western Oregon and the Sierra Nevada Mountains of California, with occasional ornamental specimens planted in the eastern United States and western Europe. They thrive on mountain slopes and the sides of canyons and ravines. The tree attains its maximum size at elevations between three and seven thousand feet, growing up to 250 feet high and 12 feet in diameter. In cultivation, however, it grows slowly, and does not attain these extreme heights. This is the largest pine, and a very valuable one on the lumber market today.

Sugar pine was so named for a sweet thick substance that is expressed from slashes in the heartwood. The wood is light red with creamy white sapwood, lightweight and with a soft texture. The grain is straight, uniform and easy to work. The sweet substance prevents the wood from rapid decay. These characteristics make it useful for shingles, construction lumber, interior finish, and especially patterns and models for metal castings.

American white pine was chosen for this corner cupboard. An aid to distinguishing American from English pine furniture is the thickness of the wood, as seen at the edges of the shelves. English furniture usually has thinner-sawn boards.

WHITE PINE

Pinus strobus

a softwood

White pine is the only soft pine that grows in the eastern United States. The heartwood is lighter brown or reddish in color than the southern hard pines, and the wood is less striped. The grain is straight, not strong, and of a soft texture. The tree grows from Newfoundland to Manitoba, southward to Pennsylvania, northern Ohio, and along the Appalachian Mountain range to Kentucky and Tennessee. The trees formerly grew in pure forests on sandy soils or small groves on fertile well-drained soil and banks of streams. The trees generally grow up to 100 feet high and 4 feet in diameter, with exceptional specimens up to 200 feet high. This is the largest conifer of the eastern forests. Since the wood is so soft and works so easily, it is used for interior moldings, lathes, matches, and the masts of ships. Lumber yards today sell many other varieties with similar wood as white pine but it probably will not be *Pinus strobus.*

New England made furniture of the 17th and 18th centuries usually has white pine as a secondary wood with hardwoods, or in painted furniture as the primary wood. When aged and oxidized, this wood becomes dull orange, hence its nickname "pumpkin pine" which is found in descriptions of early New England furniture.

This wood was exported to England in the 18th century where it was used on parts of furniture covered by gesso and gilt such as finials, swags on mirrors. To some cabinetmakers this wood is preferable to basswood (also called linden and lime), the best European wood available for this purpose.

YELLOW PINE

Pinus taeda

a softwood

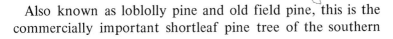

Also known as loblolly pine and old field pine, this is the commercially important shortleaf pine tree of the southern

United States forests. It grows in abundance from southern New Jersey through the eastern seaboard states to northern Florida, and west through the Gulf States. It grows in nearly pure forests, and has been successfully planted by commercial growers. At maturity the yellow pine tree stands 80 to 100 feet high and from 2 to 5 feet in diameter. The wood is coarse grained and relatively weak and brittle, but adaptable to many uses in construction. The heartwood is light brown with orange toned light sapwood.

The yellow pine wood is found as a primary and secondary wood on antique furniture from the south and is easily recognized by its distinctive light and dark striped figure on quarter swan boards.

Yellow pine was used to make this cupboard from North Carolina.

This wood was used from York County to Philadelphia as a secondary wood. Some of the Chester County inlaid pieces of furniture have this wood for a secondary wood. In lower Delaware more superb corner cupboards are made of yellow or "striped pine" and from there through the Carolinas and Georgia there are many sideboards, blanket chests, etc. of southern pine.

REDWOOD

Sequoia sempervirens

a softwood

The Indians thought they were immortal, for redwood trees have lived in pure forests for over two thousand years. None are known to have died from old age. It has now been proven that redwood trees lived all over the world with the dinosaurs, but the glaciers destroyed nearly all of them. Some of the trees that live today were saplings before Christ was born. Storms may undermine them and fires burn them, but they presumably would live forever.

These huge, tall trees, of the Pacific Coast grow 20 to 30 miles inland in Oregon and California in a belt 20 miles wide and 500 miles long. Their growth is influenced by the ocean fogs. Redwood trees are found most frequently in dense groups at the sides of ravines and banks of streams.

This tree can grow to 340 feet high, and examples are known to be 27 feet in diameter.

The heartwood is clear light red or red-brown with white sapwood. Redwood is soft, straight grained and lightweight, weighing 20 lbs. per cubic foot. This is an easy wood to work, and very resistant to decay. Therefore, it is ideal for use in contact with the soil and exterior exposure. Redwood shingles, fence posts, railway ties, green house construction furniture and water tanks are of superior quality. There is enough lumber in a single redwood tree to build 22 average homes.

If a piece of redwood is found on American antique furniture, someone is pulling your leg. This western wood was not available to the eastern colonists.

Thirty-one men and a redwood tree.

Contemporary redwood planter and hassock

ROSEWOOD
Dalbergia stevensonii
a hardwood

This exotic striped wood was, at one time, very fashionable for furniture construction. Rosewood is a tropical wood of Central and South America, with related species in India. Brazilian rosewood was favored by French cabinetmakers of the early 19th century when they referred to it as palisander, and bois de Sainte-Lucie. In Brazil, it is known as jacaranda (*D. nigra*). Whereas the Brazilian forests have been cut for generations and supplies are dwindling, the forests in Honduras are still exporting large quantities to the rest of the world. The tree can grow to 125 feet in height.

Honduras rosewood is dark red with black irregular striping that shows best when the log is cut parallel to the growth rings. The sapwood is a constrasting grey tone. The grain is straight with occasional waves, and the wood is hard, firm, and weighs 60 to 63 lbs. per cubic foot. A fragrant oil in the heartwood has the scent of rose blossoms. Because it is so hard, rosewood is difficult to work but can be polished to a high shine.

The Dutch were among the first to use rosewood for case furniture in the early 18th century. Europe soon joined in, and by the French Regency period rosewood was in great demand. Late Sheraton furniture in England also made use of the exotic, hard surface of rosewood. Today, the wood is scarce and expensive, being made into veneers usually, and piano cases.

Wood sample #19 is Honduras rosewood.

EAST INDIAN SATINWOOD

Chloroxylon swietenia

a hardwood

The blonde ribbon stripe figure of East Indian satinwood is distinctive, and has made this a favored wood for high quality furniture. An occasional plain light yellow wood log is found, but the figured ones are the rule. Since this wood is hard and brittle, it is most frequently made into veneer that can be supported by another wood, and since it is so light colored and expensive, it usually is used with contrasting woods, a small quantity at a time. The wood is very heavy weighing 58 to 62 lbs. per cubic foot.

East Indian satinwood grows primarily in Ceylon, and to a smaller extent in southern India. The trees can grow to 4 feet in diameter. European furniture makers have used this wood since the late 18th century for stringing, decorative panels, and small details. Today it is frequently found in brush and mirror backs.

Wood sample #20 is East Indian satinwood.

WEST INDIAN SATINWOOD

Zanthoxylum flavum

a hardwood

West Indian is the finest satinwood in the world, and has earned a distinguished place among hardwoods. In Great Britain it has been called Jamaican satinwood, and in the United States, San Domingan satinwood. It is all *zanthoxylum flavum*, which grows in scattered areas of southern Florida, some of the Florida Keys, the Bermuda and Bahama Islands, San Domingo and Puerto Rico. The supply in San Domingo is all but exhausted today; the commercial supply is now gathered from the other areas in very limited quantity.

This satinwood tree is not large, growing to a height of only 40 feet and 2 feet in diameter. The wood is very heavy, 55 lbs. per cubic foot, hard, brittle and with an interlocking grain of uniform or mottled figure. The color is the thing. Rich golden yellow, pale when first cut and darkening with age and exposure. This has been recognized as one of the most attractive woods and is used for the most formal furniture.

The wood must be handled carefully, for it can easily split in manufacturing, but is stable once formed. West Indian satinwood is slightly less hard than East Indian. It turns very well and can be polished to a high shine.

In the 17th century this satinwood was shipped from Bermuda to London. From that period on, it has appeared in English furniture of expensive and delicate design. Its heyday, perhaps, was the Hepplewhite and Sheraton periods, when the veneers were utilized for their full impact by imaginative designers who made use of the mottled, beautiful grain.

In America, New York and Baltimore cabinetmakers best used satinwood, often in contrast with other darker woods and shaded with hot sand to form decorative patterns.

Satinwood veneer makes up the sides and top panels of this small box, and contrasts with the dark inlayed wood. The box is English, made around 1800.

SYCAMORE

Platanus occidentalis

a hardwood

   The sycamore tree is probably best identified by its bark which is light grey and mottled, and peels off in patches in the late fall. This process exposes the smooth inner bark which seems to glow in the dark. The goblins of Halloween especially appreciate this fellow ghost of the forest.

   The sycamore tree is also known as the buttonwood and plane tree. It grows throughout the eastern United States, the largest commercial supply coming from the south today. The tree is the tallest deciduous one in the eastern forests, as it grows to an average height of 150 feet, and 10 feet in diameter. It grows well in a variety of soils and conditions, but fastest near a water supply. The sapwood is light with a pinkish cast, and the heartwood is reddish brown. The wood is moderately heavy, hard and strong, weighs 34 lbs. per cubic foot. The grain is fine, but hard to split, and has little figure but a definite flake that is exposed best on quarter sawn logs. The wood does not resist decay, so is generally unsuitable for use out of doors. It turns well and can be bent after steaming. Since it has no taste, odor or stain it is a good choice for food containers and tobacco boxes. It makes a good barrel, and especially tough chopping or butchers' blocks. Office furniture and interior home paneling is sometimes made of sycamore. Today, 5/8 inch boards are cut as drawer stock for furniture.

   Wood sample #21 is sycamore.

TEAK

Tectonia grandis

a hardwood

   Elephants are still used to haul teak from inland jungles to the waterways, and they have been trained to stack the wood in even piles. When a bell is sounded to end the day, the elephants stop their work almost before the men with them.

The teak tree grows 150 feet tall and 40 feet in diameter in southern India, Thailand, Burma and Java where a dry season alternates with monsoons in the rain forests. Difficulty obtaining the wood in dense undergrowth now far from waterways account for s the high cost of this lumber. Teak trees are so heavy that they do not float unless they are girdled several years before being cut to allow some of the moisture to escape.

The wood is light brown when first cut, with streaks of olive green or gold. The color is apt to vary to a lighter shade while the wood dries, then becomes fixed. The grain is coarse and uneven with a dull surface, but the wood is strong and heavy, weighing 40 to 45 lbs. per cubic foot when air dried. There is a mild, leathery, almost unpleasant scent to the wood when first cut. An oil substance makes the wood very durable and resistant to metal corrosion. Therefore, this is an ideal wood for boatbuilding which is one of its principal uses. The oil also resists insects, fungus, marine borers and the usual preservative treatments. Because it is so hard, both hand and machine tools are made dull quickly by teak, and it has been found useful to pre-finish the surfaces that will be glued or polished so they will hold the respective substances.

Teak has been favored in building Chinese junks, and was found to be excellent patching material by Portuguese, Dutch and British sailors. It is also well suited to contain certain chemicals for garden furniture, flooring, and heavy construction. Chinese furniture made for European supercargoes frequently was entirely of or contained teak, and expensive Chinese furniture even today may be wholly or in part made of teak.

Wood sample #22 is teak from Thailand.

TULIP POPLAR

Liriodendron tulipifera

a hardwood

Tulip poplar is variously called the tulip tree, popular tree, yellow poplar, canoe tree and whitewood. It is entirely different from Brazilian tulipwood and although many people make the mistake, should not be confused with aspens or cottonwood—which are sometimes locally called "poplar."

The tulip poplar grows quickly into a tall, straight tree, the largest native hardwood in the United States. The tree grows from southern New England, west to Wisconsin and south to Louisiana and northern Florida. It is most commonly found in deep, rich, moist soil alone and in the open. It can be over 100 feet high and 8 to 10 feet in diameter.

The wood is lightweight, soft and relatively brittle, resists warpage, and is not strong. The heartwood is light brown with yellow, green, or purple streaks, and the sapwood is creamy white. The wood weighs 28 lbs. per cubic foot.

Industrial reports indicate tulip poplar wood is used by more different industries than any other wood. It is found in many types of building construction for interior moldings, cabinetwork, door jambs, and cornices. Since the wood stains so well it can be made to resemble walnut, maple and gum. The wood is too soft to hold up well in exterior exposures, but it paints well and is found in all sorts of boatbuilding, woodenware, carving, low-priced turnings, toys and food containers. It is frequently found in wooden tobacco and cigar boxes. Sometimes these boxes are covered by a very thin veneer of cedar, or the tulip poplar wood is marked and stained to resemble Spanish cedar. The American Indian made dugout canoes from these logs—therefore, it is known as canoe wood.

The inner bark and roots of the tulip poplar possess hydrochlorate of tulipferine, an alkaloid which can be used to stimulate human hearts.

In American furniture of the antique periods, tulip poplar wood is found frequently as a stained primary wood and as a secondary wood used in conjunction with other hardwoods such as cherry, mahogany and walnut. Drawer sides, for example, of case furniture made in New Jersey and Pennsylvania frequently are tulip poplar, with white cedar drawer bottoms.

Wood sample #23 is tulip poplar wood.

The wood of the frames of upholstered furniture often are the only clues to the origin of an antique piece. This American wing chair has a poplar frame. Seat rails of American chairs are often white oak. English chairs probably would have beech frames that have even, dark, etched markings. The legs of both American and English chairs are imported mahogany.

This lovely Pennsylvania desk of the early 18th century is made of native black walnut while the sides of the interior drawers of the writing area are distinctively marked tulip poplar. The green stripe is particularly evident on this example.

AMERICAN BLACK WALNUT

Juglans nigra
a hardwood

Americans have a love affair going with this home-grown wood which has been proposed as a national tree.

Walnut's wood is highly regarded as one of the most beautiful for furniture and paneling, as it takes a wonderful finish, remains stable, and has deep natural color or can be attractively stained.

The black walnut tree gtows in the central eastern United States, not including New England, eastern South Carolina, and Georgia or Florida. The range extends west across the Mississippi River into eastern Kansas, Oklahoma and Texas. Kansas and Missouri provide the largest commercial quantities. The tree usually grows singly or in small clumps, not in thick forests. A mature tree can be 100 to 150 feet high and 4 to 6 feet in diameter in well drained soil.

The heartwood is chocolate brown, sometimes with purplish streaks, and the softwood is pale yellow. When a cut is made in the surface of finished walnut, a purple tone will be seen, whereas mahogany cuts are pink, and butternut or birch cuts are yellow. Since walnut can be stained to resemble mahogany, this cut is sometimes the only means of differentiating the two woods. Stained walnut is shown in various finishes in color plate

Walnut is a hard, strong, heavy wood that weighs 38 lbs. per cubic foot. It has good shock resistance and is unusually durable. Walnut has been so popular for furniture making that it became rare until the commercial growers planted large quantities. These planted trees are nearing maturity and available for cutting now.

The grain is coarse, but carves and works easily, and the wood holds a variety of stains well. The problems identifying finished walnut has been mentioned above, and is complicated by age and wear on antique furniture. Color plates p. 48, illustrate the close similarity old and stained surfaces can be.

Since the 17th century walnut has been shipped from Virginia to England for use in furniture. Today, examples of Vir-

173

ginia walnut can be found in Irish as well as English furniture of the 18th and 19th centuries, and sometimes can be identified only by cutting or examining the wood microscopically.

Black walnut is resistant to the furniture beetle, so the absence of its attack may be another clue that a piece of English furniture is made of American walnut. First quality wood, which is clear of knots is saved for fine furniture, and the other grades are made into gun stocks, interior paneling and veneers.

Wood sample #24 is walnut from the Missouri River Valley.

American black walnut wood was used near Philadelphia to make this drop leaf table.

EUROPEAN WALNUT

Juglans regia

a hardwood

European walnut all originated in the Circassian area of the Caucasus Mountains near the Black Sea. The Romans probably introduced it to Europe, where they planted vast quantities in England, France, Italy and Persia. Now these trees flourish in their new climates, creating wood with slight variations depending on the climate and soil conditions.

European walnut is generally lighter in color than American, the English being somewhat darker than the French. Typically, French walnut is light to dark grey brown. The grain is coarse, uniform and straight, being closer than the American. Attractive patterns can be found in striped, row, wavy and mottled figures.

The European walnut tree can grow to 100 feet high and 4 feet in diameter. The wood carves very well, and is susceptibla to larvae of the furniture beetle. Therefore, examples are found where areas have been eaten out, and only the outside shell remains. This walnut is used almost exclusively for furniture in solid or veneered forms, and very little is exported from the countries it grows in.

Wood sample #25 is figured walnut from France.

YEW

Taxus baccata
a softwood

The yew tree is a softwood native to England, but has been successfully cultivated in sections of Europe, Asia, Persia and North Africa for a long time. The tree is relatively small, standing 20 to 60 feet high, usually 3 feet in diameter but with examples 50 feet in diameter. This is a small but mighty tree that can live for over two thousand years. Superficially, the wood can be compared with American red cedar, for the color and presence of small knot holes is similar. Yew wood is orange or light tan in the heartwood and creamy white in the sapwood. The grain is compact, straight and heavy for a softwood, weighing 38 to 48 lbs. per cubic foot. This is a strong and flexible wood that was used exclusively for generations in England for archery bows.

The wood will polish to a high shine, and is resistant to the attack of the furniture beetle larvae. It has been used for many types of furniture, especially bent wood parts of Windsor chairs.

175

ZEBRAWOOD

Cynaomentra

a hardwood

   Also known as zebrano or zingana, this wood resembles the black and white stripings of a zebra. It is obtained from the west coast of Africa where the trees are large and grow in inaccessible places. The hazards encountered by native labor to obtain the lumber and transport it to water make this operation very costly. Therefore, only very limited supplies ever have been and are now available. The bark is a foot thick and is removed from the log when the tree is felled. The wood works well and finishes smoothly, making this a desirable wood for decorative borders on furniture. Especially in England in the late 18th century, zebrawood was used in veneered furniture of simple lines that set off the exotic, marked grain.

   Wood sample #26 is African zebrawood.

Carriages I

The bodywork on carriages pertained to joiners specializing in vehicles. At the moment they are making a berlin.

The Joiner

Inside the shop, one sawyer handles the ripsaw (a) and another the crosscut saw (b). At the far worktables the two-man plane (e) and brace-and-bit (d) are in use. At the left (f) a piece of parquet flooring is being finished, and completed articles of joinery stand about awaiting delivery (g, h).

GLOSSARY

Acanthus an ornamentation carved to resemble the acanthus leaves, for use on furniture and in architecture.

Annual growth ring the growth layer put on in a single growing year, including springwood and summerwood.

Back stool early term for a chair without arms.

Ball foot turned, rounded foot on furniture.

Baluster banister; an upright support of a rail, usually of a turned and vase-shaped design.

Bark outer layer of a tree, comprising the inner bark, or thin, inner living part (phloem) and the outer bark, or corky layer, composed of dry, dead tissue.

Batten strip of wood used for re-enforcement, particularly in joining two wide boards.

Beam structural member supporting a load applied transversely to it.

Bending, steam the process of forming curved wood members by steaming or boiling the wood and bending it to a form.

Bird-cage device with four balusters and a pivot placed under the top and above the shaft of a tripod table, to allow the top to be twined and tilted.

Bird's eye small localized areas in wood with the fibers indented and otherwise contorted to form few to many small circular or elliptical figures remotely resembling birds' eyes on the tangential surface. Common in sugar maple and used for decorative purposes; rare in other hardwood species.

Block foot square block of wood at the end of a plain, straight leg.

Bonnet-top pediment of broken curved design, which forms a hood topping tall case furniture.

Boss knoblike ornament used as decoration; a stud.

Bow the distortion in a board that deviates from flatness lengthwise but not across its faces.

Bracket shaped and often pierced decorative detail joining a leg and a chair seat or table top; also, a decorative shelf, or the brace upon which a shelf rests.

179

Bracket foot foot with mitered corners and unjoined sides that are often scrolled; characteristic of case furniture.

Broad-leaved trees (See *Hardwoods.*)

Broken pediment triangular or curved pediment open at the center.

Bun foot slightly flattened, circular foot with a short turned shaft.

Burl protruding, irregularly grained growth on a tree; used as a thin veneer, or made into bowls.

Cabochon a carved ornament, that surmounts a decorative motif, which can be either spherical or oval, convex or concave.

Cabriole reverse-curved leg that was popular during the Queen Anne and Chippendale periods.

Cambium the one-cell thick layer of tissue between the bark and wood that repeatedly subdivides to form new wood and bark cells.

Cant a type of bevel or chamfer.

Capital the uppermost section of a column or pilaster which crowns the shaft and supports the entablature.

Cell a general term for the minute units of wood structure, including wood fibers, vessels members, and other elements of diverse structure and function.

Chamfer the surface formed by smoothing, planing, or cutting away an angle or an edge.

180

Check a lengthwise separation of the wood, usually extending across the rings of annual growth and commonly resulting from stresset set up in the wood during seasoning.

Chinoiserie a style of decoration imitating Chinese decoration.

Chip carving a simple form of decorative carving, popular during the Middle Ages, in which patterns first prepared with compasses, are then chipped out of wooden surfaces.

Claw-and-ball a carved foot resembling a bird's claw holding a ball, commonly used as the termination of a cabriole leg in the Chippendale period.

Collapse the flattening of groups of cells in heartwood during the drying or pressure treatment of wood, characterized by a caved-in or corrugated appearance.

Cornice in architecture, the uppermost horizontal section of an entablature.

Cresting the carved decoration on the top rail of a chair, settee, day bed, or mirror.

Crook the distortion in a board that deviates edgewise from a straight line from end to end of the board.

Cross section a section of wood cut at right angles to the grain exposing the open ends of the vertical wood element.

Cross-stretcher horizontal brace in the form of an X joining the legs of chairs, tables, and case pieces.

C-scroll scroll carved in the form of the letter C.

Cup the distortion in a board that deviates flatwise from a straight line across the width of the board.

Cyma in architecture, a section of the molding of the cornice having a wavy or curved profile; an ogee.

Decay the decomposition of wood substance by fungi.

   Advanced (or typical) decay the older stage of decay in which the destruction is readily recognized because the wood has become punky, soft and spongy, stringy, ringshaked, pitted, or crumbly. Decided discoloration or bleaching of the rotted wood is often apparent.

   Incipient decay the early stage of decay that has not proceeded far enough to soften or otherwise perceptibly impair the hardness of the wood. It is usually accompanied by a slight discoloration or bleaching of the wood.

Density the weight of a body per unit volume. When expressed in the c.g.s. (centimeter-gram-second) system, it is numerically equal to the specific gravity of the same substance.

Dentils   a series of small, decorative, rectangular blocks, equally spaced and projecting as under a cornice.

Diffuse-porous wood   certain hardwoods in which the pores tend to be uniform in size and distribution throughout each annual ring or to decrease in size slightly and gradually toward the outer border of the ring.

Dimension   (See *Lumber.*)

Dimension stock   a term largely superseded by the term hardwood dimension lumber. It is hardwood stock processed to a point where the maximum waste is left at a dimension mill, and the maximum utility is delivered to the user. It is stock of specified thickness, width, and length, in multiples thereof. According to specification, it may be solid or glued; rough or surfaced; semifabricated or completely fabricated.

Dimensional stabilization   reduction through special treatment in swelling and shrinking of wood, caused by changes in its moisture content with changes in relative humidity.

Dovetail   flaring tenons (resembling a dove's tail) which interlace to form a right-angled joint.

Dry kiln   (See *Kiln.*)

Dry rot   a term loosely applied to any dry, crumbly rot but especially to that which, when in an advanced stage, permits the wood to be crushed easily to a dry powder. The term is actually a misnomer, since all wood-rotting fungi require considerable moisture for growth.

Durability   resistance to the effects of weathering and decay organisms.

Escutcheon   the shaped surface on which armorial bearings are displayed; also a decorative shield used around a keyhole to protect wood.

Early wood   (See *Springwood.*)

Edge-grained   (See *Grain.*)

Extractives   substances in wood, not an integral part of the cellular structure, that can be removed by solution in hot or cold water, ether, benzene, or other solvents that do not react chemically with wood components.

Extraneous material   foreign matter in wood which is not one of the two main constituents (cellulose and lignin) of wood. Also called infiltration products.

Fiber, wood   a comparatively lone (1/25 or less to 1/3″), narrow, tapering wood cell closed at both ends.

Fiddle-back   violin-shaped solid splat of a chair characteristic of the Queen Anne style.

Figure   the pattern produced in a wood surface by annual growth rings, rays, knots, deviations from regular grain such as interlocked and wavy grain, and irregular coloration.

Finial a crowning architectural or design detail used as a terminal ornament.

Finish wood products to be used in the joiner work, such as doors and stairs, and other fine work required to complete a building, especially the interior.

Flakes (See *Rays, wood.*)

Flat-grained (See *Grain.*)

Fluting series of half-round, parallel concave channels carved into the surface of a piece of wood.

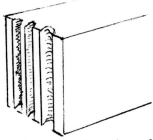

Framing lumber used for the structural members of a building, such as studs and joists.

French knot a bracket foot with an outward curve.

Fretwork ornamental openwork or work in relief with a design similar to latticework.

Gallery pierced work or balustrade forming a railing around the top of a piece of furniture.

Gateleg gatelike legs support the drop leaves of the table when open and fold against the frame of the table when closed.

Georgian term broadly used to refer to the English styles developed during the reigns of Georges I–IV, 1714–1830.

Gilt overlaid with a thin covering of gold, or a substance resembling gold.

Girder a large or principal beam used to support concentrated loads at points along its length.

Grade the designation of quality of a manufactured piece of wood or of logs.

Grain the direction, size, arrangement, appearance, or quality of the elements in wood or lumber. To have a specific meaning the term must be qualified.

   Close-grained wood wood with narrow, inconspicuous annual rings. The term is sometimes used to designate wood having small and closely spaced pores, but in this sense the term "fine textured" is more often used.

   Coarse-grained wood wood with wide conspicuous annual rings in which there is considerable difference between springwood and summerwood. The term is sometimes used to designate wood with large pores, such as oak, ash, chestnut, and walnut, but in this sense the term "coarse textured" is more often used.

Cross-grained wood   wood in which the fibers deviate from a line parallel to the sides of the piece. Cross grain may be either diagonal or spiral grain, or a combination of the two.

Curly-grained wood   wood in which the fibers are distorted so that they have a curled appearance, as in "bird's-eye" wood. The areas showing curly grain may vary up to several inches in diameter.

Diagonal-grained wood   wood in which the annual rings are at an angle with the axis of a piece as a result of sawing at an angle with the bark of the tree or log. A form of cross grain.

Edge-grained lumber   lumber that has been sawed so that the wide surfaces extend approximately at right angles to the annual growth rings. Lumber is considered edge grained when the rings form an angle of 45° to 90° with the wide surface of the piece.

Fine-grained wood   (See *Grain, close-grained wood.*)

Flat-grained lumber   lumber that has been sawed so the wide surfaces extend approximately parallel to the annual growth rings. Lumber is considered flat grained when the annual growth rings make an angle of less than 45° with the surface of the piece.

Interlocked-grained wood   wood in which the fibers are inclined in in one direction in a number of rings of annual growth, then gradually reverse and are inclined in an opposite direction in succeeding growth rings, then reverse again.

Open-grained wood   common classification by painters for woods with large pores, such as oak, ash, chestnut, and walnut. Also known as "coarse textured."

Plainsawed lumber   another term for flat-grained lumber.

Quartersawed lumber   another term for edge-grained lumber.

Spiral-grained wood   wood in which the fibers take a spiral course about the trunk of a tree instead of the normal vertical course. The spiral may extend in a right-handed or left-handed direction around the tree trunk. Spiral grain is a form of cross grain.

Straight-grained wood   wood in which the fibers run parallel to the axis of a piece.

Vertical-grained lumber   another term for edge-grained lumber.

Wavy-grained wood   wood in which the fibers collectively take the the form of waves or undulations.

Green   freshly sawed lumber, or lumber that has received no intentional drying; unseasoned. The term does not apply to lumber that may have become completely wet through waterlogging.

Goldleaf an extremely thin leaf of gold used for gilding.

Growth ring an area of wood composed of summerwood and spring-wood. In softwoods, the summerwood is darker in color and more prominent because of its formation of larger pores.

Hardwoods Generally, the botanical group of trees that have broad leaves, in contrast to the conifers or softwoods. The term has no reference to the actual hardness of the wood.

Herringbone inlay made of veneer cut obliquely and fitted together in a herringbone pattern.

Heartwood the wood extending from the pith to the sapwood, the cells of which no longer participate in the life processes of the tree. Heartwood may be infiltrated with gums, resins, and other materials that usually make it darker and more decay resistant than sapwood.

Highboy high chest of drawers set upon a lower case of drawers on ta-blelike legs.

Honeycombing checks, often not visible at the surface, that occur in the interior of a piece of wood, usually along the wood rays.

Inlay decoration attained by setting contrasting materials into the body of a surface.

Intaglio an incised design, depressed below the surface of the material; opposed to cameo or relief.

Japanning to lacquer or cover with a coat of japan or other varnish having similar properties of hardness and brilliance.

Joint the junction of two pieces of wood or veneer.

Joist one of a series of parallel beams used to support floor and ceil-ing loads and supported in turn by larger beams, girders, or bearing walls.

Kiln heated chamber for drying lumber, veneer, and other wood prod-ucts.

Knot that portion of a branch or limb which has been surrounded by subsequent growth of the wood of the trunk or other portion of the tree. As a knot appears on the sawed surface, it is merely a section of the entire knot, its shape depending upon the direction of the cut.

Kas large cupboard in the Dutch style, usually with a heavy overhang-ing cornice.

Lacquer spirit varnish put on wood in many layers to build up a hard, highly polished surface.

Lamb's-tongue a geometric shape formed by the terminus (resembling a lamb's tongue) of a chamfer.

Longitudinal generally, the direction along the length of the grain of wood.

Lowboy modern term for a dressing table with small drawers, mounted on legs.

Lumber the product of the saw and planing mill, not further manufactured than by sawing, resawing, passing lengthwise through a standard planing machine, cross-cutting to length, and matching.

Boards yard lumber less than 2″ thick and 1 or more inches wide.

Dimension lumber from 2″ to, but not including 5″ thick, and 2 or more inches wide.

Dressed size the dimensions of lumber after shrinking from the green dimensions and being surfaced with a planing machine to usually 3/8 or 1/2″ less than the nominal or rough size. For example, a 2 × 4″ stud actually measures 1-5/8 × 3-5/8″ under American lumber standards for softwood lumber.

Nominal size as applied to timber or lumber, the rough-sawed commercial size by which it is known and sold in the market.

Structural lumber lumber that is 2 or more inches thick and 4 or more inches wide, intended for use where working stresses are required. The grading of structural lumber is based on the strength of the piece and the use of the entire piece.

Timbers lumber 5 or more inches in least dimension. Timbers may be classified as beams, stringers, posts, caps, sills, girders, purlins, etc.

Marbleize to paint an imitation of marble.

Marlborough leg leg of square section with a blocked foot, used for Chippendale chairs and tables.

Marquetry decorative inlay in which the pattern is formed of various woods before being glued to a groundwork.

Medullary rays (See *Rays, wood.*)

Millwork generally, all building materials made of finished wood and manufactured in millwork plants and planing mills. Includes such items as inside and outside doors, window and door frames, blinds, porch work, mantels, panel work, stairways, moldings, and interior trim. Does not include flooring, ceiling, or siding.

Moisture content of wood the amount of water contained in the wood. Usually expressed as a percentage of the weight of the ovendry wood.

Miter (mitre) the diagonal joint in a molding formed by the two pieces of woodwork intersecting at right angles.

Mortise and tenon the joining of two pieces of material, usually wood, by the insertion of one piece (the tenon) into the cavity or socket (the mortise) of the other.

Molding a decorative band that is obtained by a continuous projection or incision applied to a surface.

  Bead a molding with a surface consisting of small, round, projecting shapes.

  Bead-and-reel round, convex molding or turning alternating oval beads and disks.

  Bolection molding with a bold, projecting surface.

  Cavetto concave molding, usually one-quarter round.

  Cock bead a projecting molding that consists of small, half-round sections; usually applied to drawer fronts.

  Cove a large, concave molding generally applied to cornices.

  Egg-and-dart repeating convex molding with a design resembling an egg and a dart.

  Ogee a molding having an S-shaped profile.

  Quarter-round an ovolo; the name in both architecture and cabinet-making for a convex molding precisely quarter round in section.

  Scratch bead a simulated beading formed by a scratch or continuous indentation along the edge of a board.

  Step a molding with a cross-section resembling steps.

  Thumb a convex molding with a flat curve that resembles the profile of a thumb.

Naval stores a term applied to the oils, resins, tars, and pitches derived from oleoresin contained in, exuded by, or extracted from trees chiefly of the pine species (genus *Pinus*) or from the wood of such trees.

Ogee (See *Cyma and Molding.*)

Old growth timber growing in or harvested from a mature, naturally established forest. When the trees have grown moist or all of their individual lives in active competition with their companions for sunlight and moisture, this timber is usually straight and relatively free of knots.

Ovendry wood wood dried to constant weight in an oven at temperatures above that of boiling water (usually 101° to 105°C. or 214° to 221°F.).

Pad foot oval-shaped foot on cabriole legs.

Patera small carved or inlaid ornaments either oval or round, used in the decoration of such items as friezes, mirror crestings, and chair splats.

Patina the surface of woods mellowing in color and finish, from age or use.

Pediment a triangular feature at the top of a portico or a cabinet.

Peck pockets or areas of disintegrated wood caused by advanced stages of localized decay in the living tree. It is usually associated with cypress and incense-cedar. There is no further development of peck once the lumber is seasoned.

Pilaster an upright rectangular member, structurally a pier, but architecturally treated as a column.

Pinnate leaves characterized by the division of the leaflets, or primary sections, onto each side of a common leafstalk, or extension of a leafstalk.

Pitch pocket an opening that extends parallel to the annual growth rings and that contains, or has contained, either solid or liquid pitch.

Pitch streak a well-defined accumulation of pitch in a more or less regular streak in the wood of certain softwoods.

Pith the small, soft core occurring in the structural center of a tree trunk, branch, twig, or log.

Plainsawed (See *Grain.*)

Planing-mill products products worked to pattern, such as flooring, ceiling, and siding.

Plate rail a primitive flat rail characterized by a raised outer edge.

Plinth the lowest section of a base, or a block serving as a base for objects such as urns, bases, or statues.

Plywood an assembly made of layers (plies) of veneer, or of veneer in combination with a lumber core, joined with an adhesive. The grain of adjoining plies is usually laid at right angles, and almost always an odd number of plies are used to obtain balanced construction.

Pore a vessel found in hardwoods. In a cross section pores appear as open holes and in many species they can be seen without the aid of a hand lens if the wood is cut cleanly.

Porous woods another name for hardwoods, which frequently have vessels or pores large enough to be seen readily without magnification.

Preservative any substance that is effective, for a reasonable length of time, in preventing the development and action of wood-rotting fungi, borers of various kinds, and harmful insects that deteriorate wood.

Quarter-round molding (See *Molding.*)

Quartersawed (See *Grain.*)

Radial in studying wood the radial surface is that which is produced by cutting parallel to the grain and in such a way that the knife blade is pointed toward the log center—like a spoke in a wheel. This is the direction in which the wood rays grow.

Ray a straight pencil-like line of cells extending in a radial direction across the grain. Rays vary in height from a few cells in some species to 4 or more inches in oak. The size is of importance in identifying a a wood. The rays serve primarily to store food and transport it horizontally in the tree.

Rate of growth the rate at which a tree has laid on wood, measured radially in the trunk or in lumber cut from the trunk. The unit of measure in use is number of annual growth rings per inch.

Reeding parallel, semicircular molding which protrudes from the surface.

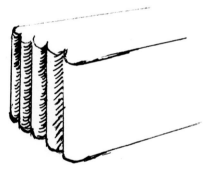

Relief decoration raised above the surface.

Resin passage (or duct) intercellular passages that contain and transmit resinous materials. They may extend vertically parallel to the axis of the tree or at right angles to the axis and parallel to the rays. Resin ducts look like dark gummy streaks on the side grain of some woods, such as sugar pine.

Ring-porous woods a group of hardwoods in which the pores are comparatively large at the beginning of each annual ring and decrease in size more or less abruptly toward the outer portion of the ring, thus forming a distinct inner zone of pores, known as the springwood, and an outer zone with smaller pores, known as the summerwood.

Sap all the fluids in a tree except special secretions and excretions, such as oleoresin.

Sapwood the outer part of the wood in a log—just inside the bark. It is lighter in color than the heartwood.

Scratch bead molding (See *Molding.*)

Scroll pediment a pediment formed by two separate confronting cyma curves; also called a broken-scroll.

Seasoning removing moisture from green wood in order to improve its serviceability.

  Air-dried dried by exposure to air, usually in a yard, without artificial heat.

  Kiln-dried dried in a kiln with the use of artificial heat.

Second growth timber that has grown after removal by cutting, fire, wind, or other agency, of all or a large part of the previous stand.

Serpentine resembling a serpent or having a winding, turning surface.

Skirt the horizontal piece of wood below a table top, chair seat, or underframing of a case piece; frequently carved, pierced, or scalloped.

Slipper foot a slender foot, pointed and extended.

Slip seat also known as "loose seat"; the separate upholstered wood frame that is let into the framing of the chair seat.

Snake foot elongated foot shaped like a snake's head.

Softwood wood produced from needle-bearing trees. The term does not refer to the softness of the wood. Also known as "nonporous" wood.

Spade foot a tapered rectangular foot having a spade-shaped profile.

Spandrel a usually triangular element that is used for decorative purposes in a corner, or corners.

Spanish foot a scroll foot having vertical rib designs within the scroll curve.

Spindle a slender turning used primarily in a chair back for support. See *Turnings* for illustration.

Splat an upright, single center support of a chair back having flat, thin features.

Spool turning (See *Turning.*)

Springwood a portion of an annual growth ring which is produced at the beginning of a growing season. In hardwoods, the springwood is characterized by a line of pores. In softwoods, by a light colored area of tracheids.

Stain a discoloration in wood that may be caused by such diverse agencies as microorganisms, metal, or chemicals. The term also applies to materials used to color wood.

Step molding (See *Molding.*)

Stile an upright side support in a chair back.

Sterngth the term in its broader sense includes all the properties of wood that enable it to resist different forces or loads. In its more restricted sense, strength may apply to any one of the mechanical properties, in which event the name of the property under consideration should be stated, thus: strength in compression parallel to grain, strength in bending, hardness, and so on.

Stress force per unit of area.

Stretcher the rungs that connect the legs of chairs and tables.

  Box the stretchers that connect the legs in a 4-sided pattern.

  Cross the X-shaped horizontal brace which connects the diagonal legs.

  H the stretcher construction in which side stretchers from the front to the back legs are connected through the middle by a third piece.

Stud one of a series of slender wood structural members used as supporting elements in walls and partitions.

Summerwood the part of a growth ring produced late in the growing season. In softwoods it appears as a darker colored line of tracheids. In hardwoods the summerwood is composed of densely packed small pores.

Tangential the tangential surface of wood is that which is at right angles to the radial surface. Flat-grained and plainsawed lumber is sawed tangentially.

Texture a term which refers to the relative size and amounts of wood elements which determine its appearance, feel and cutting characteristics. A coarse-textured wood could be compared to a piece of burlap, in contrast to a fine-textured wood which would be likened to silk.

Tracheids the principal cells found in softwoods. They resemble many closely-packed, open-end tubes, one over the other, when viewed on a smoothly-cut end surface with a hand lens.

Treen small domestic objects made of wood.

Trestle foot rectangular blocks of wood extending from each side of the end of table leg in order to provide better stability.

Trifid foot three-toed; also called a drake foot.

Trompe l'oeil any form of decoration that can deceive or "fool-the-eye" of the beholder.

Turning an ancient craft of woodworking in which cutting tools are applied to a rotating surface.

Turning (continued)

    Ball spherical turnings; usually in a series.

    Disc turnings which resemble a disc or discus in profile.

    Ring turnings giving the appearance of a flattened ball turning.

    Spool a series of bulbous turnings that resemble rows of spools.

    Trumpet a turned leg having the profile of an upturned trumpet.

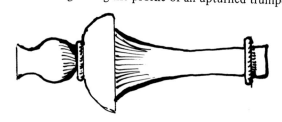

    Vase a turning resembling a vase, with a bulbous base beneath a taper shape.

Twist a distortion caused by the turning or winding of the edges of a board so that the four corners of any face are no longer in the same plane.

Tyloses masses of cells appearing somewhat like froth in the pores of some hardwoods, notably white oak and black locust. In hardwoods, tyloses are formed when walls of living cells surrounding vessels extend into the vessels. They are sometimes formed in softwoods in a similar manner by the extension of cell walls into resin-passage cavities.

Veneer a thin layer or sheet of wood cut on a veneer machine.

    Rotary-cut veneer veneer cut in a lathe which rotates a log or bolt, chucked in the center, against a knife.

    Sawed veneer veneer produced by sawing.

    Sliced veneer veneer that is sliced off a log, bolt, or flitch with a knife.

Vertical grain (See *Grain.*)

Vessels wood cells of comparatively large diameter that have open ends and are set one above the other so as to form continuous tubes. The openings of the vessels on the surface of a piece of wood are usually referred to as pores.

Virgin growth the original growth of mature trees.

Volute an ornament with a spiral or rolled-up conformation.

Wainscot the modern designation for the panel back chair; or any chair of solid construction.

Wane bark or lack of wood from any cause on the edge or corner of a piece of lumber.

Warp any variation from a true or plane surface. Warp includes bow, crook, cup, and twist, or any combination thereof.

Weathering the mechanical or chemical disintegration and discoloration of the surface of wood that is caused by exposure to light, the action of dust and sand carried by winds, and the alternate shrinking and swelling of the surface fibers with the continual variation in moisture content brought by changes in the weather. Weathering does not include decay.

Wood substance the solid material of which wood is composed. It usually refers to the extractive-free solid substance of which the cell walls are composed, but this is not always true. There is no wide variation in chemical composition or specific gravity between the wood substance of various species; the characteristic differences of species are largely due to differences in infiltrated materials and variations in relative amounts of cell walls and cell cavities.

Workability the degree of ease and smoothness of cut obtainable with hand or machine tools.

Yoke the term applied to the crest rail of a chair back.

Picture Credits

American Forestry Institute, 95 (bottom), 116; American Plywood Association, 37, 38, 39 (center); Atheneum of Philadelphia, 61; Broughton Lumber Company, 90 (top); California Redwood Association, 20, 83, 84 (top), 123, 164, 165; Caterpillar Tractor Company, 120 (top), 103 (top, bottom); Champion International Corporation, 22, 26, 28 (bottom), 39 (top, bottom), 62 (bottom), 95 (top), 96, 98, 115; Design Research, Cover, 74, 75, 122; Diderot, Denis, Encyclopedia, viii, 10, 24, 40, 77; Food and Agriculture Organization of the United Nations, v, 87, 88, 89 (bottom right), 93 (bottom), 100 (center), 104, 105, 106, 107, 108, 109, 110 (top), 121 (center left), 121 (bottom right), 124, 148, 150, 177; Hardwood Plywood Products, 31; Walter Himmelreich, 60 (bottom); Charlotte Horstmann Ltd., 22 (left); Alan McIlvain Company, 22 (right), 43, 45, 47, 49, 51, 53, 55, 57, 86, 89 (bottom left), 111, 112, 117, 118, 119; Mead Paper Company, 99 (bottom), 100 (bottom), 103 (center left); Museum of English Rural Life, 76, 81, 84 (bottom), 85 (bottom), 120 (left), 121 (top left), 121 (bottom right), 130; Pennsylvania Bureau of Forestry, 32 (bottom), 85 (top), 89 (top), 90 (bottom), 94, 97, 99 (top), 101, 126, 158; publisher's file, 15; Gordon Saltar, 78, 79; Herbert F. Schiffer, 13, 25, 27, 28 (top), 29, 30, 62 (top), 63, 113, 114; Herbert Schiffer Antiques, Inc., Cover, 32 (top), 33, 35, 59, 60 (top), 64, 66, 67, 68, 69, 70, 71, 72, 73, 135, 138, 152, 154, 157, 160, 162, 167, 171, 172, 174; Schiffer Limited, 17, 19, 21, 23, 42, 44, 46, 48, 50, 52, 54, 56; Western Wood Products Association, i, ii, iii, iv, 91, 92 (bottom, center), 93 (top, center), 143; Weyerhaeuser Corporation, 30 (bottom), 82, 92 (top), 100 (top), 103 (center right), 110 (bottom), 120 (right), 121 (top right), 121 (center right), 144; Wycombe Chair Museum. 132.

Bibliography

Andrews, Ralph W.
Timber, toil and trouble in the big woods. Superior Publishing Co., 1968, Bonanza Books, Crown Publishers, Inc., New York.

Appalachian Hardwood Year Book, 1976-77, Appalachian Hardwood Manufacturers, Inc., High Point, N.C.

Bining, Arthur Cecil
Iron Manufacture in the Eighteenth Century. Pa. Historical Commission. Vol IV, Harrisburg, 1938, p. 75.

Brown, H. P., Panshin, A. J., Forsaith, C. C.
Textbook of Wood Technology, Vol I, II, III, N.Y., McGraw-Hill Book Co. Inc., 1952

Buyer's Manual, 1974, Southeastern Lumber Manufacturers Association, College Park, Georgia.

Champion International Corporation, annual reports 1975, 1976, Stamford, Conn.

Constantine, Albert, Jr., revised by Harry J. Hobbs
Know Your Woods, Charles Scribner & Sons, N.Y., 1975.

Diderot, Denis
Encyclopedia of Trades and Industry, Dover Publications, Inc., N.Y. 2 vol., 1959

Edlin, Herbert L.
What Wood Is That?, Viking Press, N.Y., 1977

Food and Agriculture Organization of the United Nations. *Logging and log transport in tropical high forest.* Rome, 1974

Green, Henry D.
Furniture of the Georgia Piedmont before 1830. The High Museum of Art, Atlanta, 1976

Hinckley, F. Lewis
Directory of the Historic Cabinet Woods. A complete guide to all hardwoods used in furniture making 1460-1900. Crown Publishers, Inc., New York, N.Y. 1960

Holcombe, Robert A.
Wood Study Kit Manual, Timber Engineering Company, Washington, 1956

Horst, Mel, and Smith, Elmer L.
Logging in the Pennsylvania north woods. Applied Arts Publishers, Lebanon, Pa., 1969

Imported Wood Purchasing Guide, second edition, International Wood Trade Publications, Inc., Memphis, Tenn., 1974

The International Book of Wood, New York, Simon & Schuster, 1976

Jane, F. W.

The Structure of Wood, New York, Macmillan, 1956

Marsh, William Barton

Philadelphia Hardwood, 1798–1948, William E. Ridge's Sons, 1948

Neelands, R. W.

Important Trees of Eastern Forests. U.S. Dept. of Agriculture—Forest Service, Western Publishing Company, Inc., 1968

Sargent, Charles Sprague

Manual of the Trees of North America (exclusive of Meixco) 2nd corrected edition in 2 vols., New York, Dover Publications, Inc. © 1965 (first © 1905)

Schiffer, Herbert F. and Peter B. Schiffer

Miniature Antique Furniture, Livingston Publishing Company, Wynnewood, Pa. 1972

Sparkes, Ivan G.

Woodland Craftsmen, Shire Publications, Ltd., Bucks, U.K., 1977

Van Ravensway, Charles

A Checklist of the Pines of North America

Wood Colors and Kinds. U.S. Dept. of Agriculture, Handbook No. 101, 1956

198

201